AN ARMY OF
ORDINARY
PEOPLE

Other books written by
Tony and Felicity Dale:

Renewing the Mind

Simply Church

Getting Started
*A Practical Guide to
House Church Planting*

AN ARMY OF
ORDINARY
PEOPLE

Real stories of ordinary people advancing God's Kingdom

BY FELICITY DALE

AN ARMY OF ORDINARY PEOPLE

Published in Austin, Texas, by Karis Publishing, Inc.

Karis Publishing, Inc.
1011 Meredith Drive, Suite 10
Austin, TX 78748 USA

ISBN: 0-9718040-6-0

Printed in the United States of America

WHAT OTHERS ARE SAYING...

"In her book, *An Army of Ordinary People*, Felicity Dale reminds us that God uses common, everyday people to extend His Kingdom. Felicity has written in the language of the common man, relating with every one of us who desire to have a meaningful walk with God. She shares real stories of regular folks that God is using to infect their communities with the love, care and compassion of Christ. This book will allow everyone to relate with 'life in Christ.' It's simple; anyone can do it! I highly recommend it!"

Rev. Michael Steele, *Dawn Ministries, North American Director*

"This book is a pearl. Felicity adds layer upon layer in the form of personal stories of 'ordinary' people from a wide range of backgrounds, each used by God. The final product is a pearl of great beauty and luster. Each example demonstrates how God can miraculously transform lives and advance His Kingdom, making pearls out of 'ordinary' grains of sand given to His loving hands."

Curtis Sergeant, *Director of Church Planting, Saddleback Church*

"This book is a forecast of what church will look like for many in the emerging generation: A missional church without walls where every Christ follower is discipled in the Great Commandment and empowered in the Great Commission. Put these stories in the hands of young people and watch them make history for God!"

Jaeson Ma, *Campus Church Networks*

"A man or woman with a God story is not the prisoner of someone else's theory of church. The power of the stories told in this book is that they are true, they are happening now, and they are taking place all over the world. God is up to something and I don't want to miss it!"

Floyd McClung, *All Nations Family*

"Tony & Felicity Dale are the real deal. When they speak, I listen. What they are teaching, the church as a whole must get. I am obsessed with the Kingdom and so are they. They move far beyond structural issues to core issues of how the body of Christ operates. Every church must be a 'simple church,' regardless of structure. There is so much that they bring to the whole body. My biggest fear is that pastors who have buildings—like me—will not hear what they're saying because the form is different. Forget the form. Study the function and implement it in your context and watch God move in powerful ways!"

Bob Roberts, *Senior Pastor, Northwood Church*

"Did Jesus really mean it when he said, 'The meek shall inherit the earth?' After a church-age of famous names and an ecclesial version of Fortune 500, it seems that the future of God's Kingdom is being firmly placed by God in the hands of ordinary people made extraordinary by God. In *An Army of Ordinary People*, Felicity makes this exciting process transparent and very tangible and gives faces to it. I doubt if God might have other plans for you than becoming his hero, too."

Wolfgang Simson, *Author,* ***Houses That Change the World***

"The age of the ordained has passed; welcome to the day of the ordinary. God delights in using ordinary people to do extraordinary things because it reveals His own power and glory. This book opens a window to reveal how God is already on the move in North America. My hope is that you will be so enthused after reading this book, that you will go out and do something worthy of placement in the next volume!"

Neil Cole, *Church Multiplication Associates*
Author: ***Organic Church, Cultivating a Life for God, TruthQuest***

"This book is not a theoretical treatise, but a record of real and helpful experiences. The stories in this book are empowering and affirming. The principles that flow out of each chapter are simple enough to be replicated and contextualized. This volume is a little gem. Thank you, Felicity, for giving us a vision and the faith to walk down the 'Church Planting Movement' pathway as well."

Tony Collis, *Followers Network*

ACKNOWLEDGEMENTS

Several people helped me by reading through the manuscript and giving their comments. John White and Matthew Dale worked with me from the beginning. Julie Ross, Kevin Sutter, Jeff Gilbertson, Neil and Dana Gamble, Amy Dale and Jamie Maxfield all read the manuscript and gave me helpful insights and comments. Andy Williams did a great job editing it, and Jon Dale helped with the technical side. My thanks, too, go to Mike Lyons for the cover design and electronic production of this book.

My husband, Tony, is my best friend and the love of my life. He has been an unfailing source of support and encouragement. I could not have written this book without him.

TABLE OF CONTENTS

FOREWORD by RALPH MOORE   x.

PREFACE   xii.

INTRODUCTION   xiii

HANK'S STORY	God uses ordinary people to do the extraordinary	1
TONY & FELICITY'S STORY	What is church?	9
KENNY'S STORY	The 10:2b virus	31
ELIZABETH'S STORY	The Great Commission	45
JOSH'S STORY	Bearing much fruit	61
ROSA – A PERSON OF PEACE	Luke 10 principles	77
FRANK'S STORY	The Holy Spirit leads us	89
SAM'S STORY	" Good soil."	99
DAVID'S STORY	"I will build My church"	119
LISA'S STORY	Church is built on relationships	131
THOMAS & MARIE'S STORY	Church is family	145
JOE'S STORY	The Kingdom at work	157
STUDENT STORIES	Service and strategy	169
KRISTIN'S STORY	Stone soup church	181
NEIL'S STORY	Discipleship and training	191
JIM & CATHY'S STORY	Kingdom finances and Kingdom kids	207
ALLEN'S STORY	To transition or not to transition?	219
LES'S STORY	"No empire building, no control, and no glory"	231
TONY & FELICITY'S STORY (Part 2)	The bigger picture	243
APPENDIX		253
AUTHOR BIOGRAPHY		262

FOREWORD

by Ralph Moore

How hard can it be to spend an afternoon reading a book, then write a couple of hundred words covering a few nice things you want to say? Plenty hard when the Holy Spirit uses that manuscript to align and synchronize just about everything you've been thinking for the past three years. That is my experience with Felicity Dale's *An Army of Ordinary People*. The book you hold in your hand is too refreshing to introduce in two or three pages. I wish I could write a whole book about it.

I ordinarily pull a few quotes from a manuscript then write a forward around the author's words. After reading Ordinary People, I found that I had copied 17 pages of quotes. It is no stretch to say that this book grabbed me by the shirt, shook me up and set me down facing a new direction. Let me be clear; I don't mean to say that I experienced a "paradigm shift." Far, far better than that, a half dozen loosely related passions and hunches fell into place that afternoon. I spent the better part of the next two days alternating between brooding over what I had read and trumpeting its values to everyone in talking distance.

Felicity Dale gave me a new set of tools through her carefully crafted collection of stories. It's been said too often of too many books but I'll take the risk: "This book reads like the twenty-ninth chapter of Acts." I take that back—"It reads like chapters 29-36."

The book taught me why I should not attempt to transform our "legacy church" to a collection of house churches—our people didn't sign up for that, so leave them in peace. It underscores the necessity of prayer-evangelism to the formulating of new congregations. It champions the power of the Spirit to work through ordinary and untrained (seminary, etc.) people to lead the church. It shows how quickly the field can produce its own workers and resources. In other words, there is little cost in planting house churches, leaving open the possibility that we could quadruple or quintuple the speed of our church-planting efforts. I learned, from a new angle, the importance of finding and working with the person of peace. I even discovered why Jesus said to remain in one home (Luke 10) and why door-to-door evangelism is so difficult, even futile.

I lead a cell-based church and thoroughly believe in our approach. We've planted more than 300 congregations through our model and are looking toward 1,000. My problem is that I have been unable to connect our current model to the power of the house church movement. Add to this mix my impatience with those who imply that meeting in houses represents the "holy grail," discounting or discarding those who disagree with them. Meanwhile I've been looking for keys to be myself, fulfill my calling and respond to an obvious new move of the Holy Spirit. I found several of those keys between the covers of this book.

Ralph Moore
Founding Pastor, Hope Chapels
Author, **Starting a New Church**

PREFACE

Writing this book has been both a privilege and a humbling experience for me. When I first announced the idea of a book of stories that would illustrate house or simple church principles, I had no idea the journey I would take. I have spent many hours talking with the people whose lives are portrayed here, and was often profoundly moved and challenged by what I heard.

Some of the names in the stories have been changed, for reasons which will become obvious.

This book is not aimed at theologians. Instead, it is written for ordinary people like the ones whose stories are told here. My hope is that anyone reading this book will gain a vision to join the ranks of an army of people who, with outrageous faith, have dared to take God at His word, make disciples and thereby join Him in building His church.

This book is not for the religious or faint-hearted. It will offend those who prefer not to cross paths with people who aren't "just like me." This book is for those who are in the trenches, willing to get their hands dirty in the pain and glory of life. It is for those who aren't afraid to go where Jesus did; it is for people who are willing to risk letting God be God and to do things His way...Enjoy!

My thanks go to everyone who was willing to risk opening their lives to share their story.

This book belongs to them.

Felicity Dale
Austin, Texas
August 2005

INTRODUCTION

This is a book of stories. Stories are compelling; they grab you. Jesus used stories to illustrate spiritual principles again and again. He told stories people could relate to—stories about things with which His hearers would be familiar. People will remember our stories even if they forget everything else we say.

Each of the stories in this book is about the life of an ordinary person God has used to make disciples and start a simple church. You will notice that very few of the people are in so-called "full-time ministry." Most of them are like you and me—they get up in the morning and go to work all day. They raise families. They have their share of problems and frustrations. They are not spiritual superstars.

But something happens when they make the decision to reach out to unbelievers to make disciples and start a church. All of a sudden, their stories make a wild shift into the extraordinary! God seems more than willing to accept their offer to yield their life to Him. He then turns their lives—and their world—upside down.

Across the nations, God is speaking the same message to people. He no longer wants it to be church as usual. He wants His church back! Everywhere, people are catching a vision of a church that is simpler, that meets around the dining table in a home, or in an office or a coffee house. It is a vibrant community, based on building relationships and following the leading of the Holy Spirit.

An army of anonymous people—"nameless and faceless"—is rising up. They are willing to take God at His word and attempt to reach their world with the good news that Jesus still opens blind eyes and sets captives free. Under the command of their Captain, they are following Him wherever He leads. And He is taking them into unexplored territory where the lost are waiting to hear about Life and have their lives transformed by Him. Then Jesus is challenging them to gather this "new wine" into the new wineskins of small, caring communities of His people, which He calls church. He promises that His presence will be there with them.

Each story illustrates a principle (or two) about how to make disciples that become a simple church. My hope and prayer in writing this book is that anyone reading it can identify with one of the stories and say, "I can do that!"

HANK'S STORY

God uses ordinary people to do the extraordinary

JUST AN ORDINARY GUY...

Hank is an ordinary kind of guy. Introverted and unassuming, his friends used to joke that it was a real achievement if they could get him to say three words. He didn't go to college or seminary, and he's not a pastor. After graduating from high school, Hank went into the military. At the time this story begins, Hank managed the produce section of a large grocery store.

Hank's spiritual life recently had been revitalized when a friend found out he was no longer attending a traditional church, and he invited Hank to visit his church that met in a home. While there, he reconnected with Doug. Doug was a friend from years ago when he and Hank played in the worship band at a local church. He now was a pastor of a traditional church, as well as the one who led the group that met in a home.

"A couple of us guys get together at Starbucks every week. We read some chapters out of the Bible during the week. Then on Fridays we get together to hold each other accountable for what is going on in our lives and to pray for our friends. We call it a Life Transformation Group. Would you like to join us?" Doug asked him.

So began the transformation in Hank's life. Each week, the three of them would devour whole books of the Bible. Over coffee they would confess areas of their lives in which they struggled, and pray for their non-Christian friends. And things started happening.

The first was devastating. Hank's wife of more than 20 years left and then divorced him. It was a tough time. At this point, Hank chose to throw himself even more vigorously into what the Lord was doing in his life, and he began growing spiritually like wildfire.

"I'm not sure what's going on," Hank admitted to Doug one day. "At work, for no reason that I can see, some of the other employees keep asking me to pray for them. They never used to do that. There are others around who are much more vocal about their faith than I am, but I'm the one they confide in. What do you think is going on?"

"Do you remember from our *Experiencing God* Bible study," Doug said, "that we need to see what God is doing and join Him in it? I think God is doing this. I wonder what He has in mind."

Hank asked some of the people at his workplace if they would like to start a house church. Only one of them said yes, but several of his family members (he has grown children) and some of their friends—the majority of whom were unbelievers—asked if they could also participate. So Hank started his first church. People began experiencing remarkable transformation, as one by one they gave their hearts to the Lord.

Two months later at work, Hank tripped over a hose on the ground while he was carrying a large, heavy pallet. His ankle was shattered and broken in three places, and he was confined to bed for three months. But he was so spiritually hungry during his enforced rest, all he did was pray and read his Bible and other Christian books. His new church met around him in his small apartment.

One day during his recovery, his mother asked if he would be willing to start a church in her house in a community about 20 miles away. Hank comes from a large family—he has 15 brothers and sisters. Many of them and their children joined in this new church. A month later, some of his grown children who had never been involved in church, asked if he would do something similar in their home.

Three months later, one of Hank's kids who was coming to this latest church, met a lady who was interested in talking about spiritual things. She became very excited about the concept of home church. She called Hank on the phone.

"I met your son the other day, and he was telling me about how you run churches in people's homes," she said. "I would love to have something like that in my home. Would you be willing to show me how?" So a fourth church started. That simple church has grown and spawned several other groups that are in the process of becoming churches.

Six churches now meet in homes that are traceable to Hank, the guy people teased because he never said anything!

... WHO HAS AN EXTRAORDINARY GOD

Other amazing things have happened to Hank. He and two other people went to visit Jose, a friend who was in a coma in the hospital following a suicide attempt. (Jose, a 21-year-old, had been heavily involved in gangs and drugs most of his life.) When they went to the ICU at the hospital, a group of doctors were gathered around Jose's bed, preparing permission forms to harvest Jose's organs. Their patient was brain-dead, and they had just pulled the plug on the life-support machines. The grieving relatives were waiting in the hallway.

"Why don't we pray for him anyway?" one of the friends asked. "Then we can go out for a bite to eat and come back later."

The small group of believers gathered around the bedside, laid their hands on the brain-dead man and prayed: "Lord, when You walked this earth, You healed the sick and raised the dead! Will You come and show Your power again in this situation?"

When they retuned to the ICU some time later, there was a lot of activity and an air of suppressed excitement. They wondered what all the commotion was about. Then one of the boy's relatives came up to them with tears streaming down his cheeks.

"You will not believe what has just happened," he exclaimed, amazement written all over his face. "Shortly after you left, Jose opened his eyes. The doctors could not believe it. All their tests showed that he was dead. Look at him now!"

Hank and the others went into the ICU. Jose was sitting up in bed, eating a Popsicle.

On another occasion, Hank prayed for a girl with a serious brain tumor, and she was healed. Hank has grown into a man of faith. He knows beyond any shadow of doubt that God heals the sick and raises the dead.

But there is something else you need to know about Hank. A few years ago, Hank was diagnosed with Lou Gehrig's disease, a condition that causes progressive loss of muscle control. For some time, he had been having difficulty performing simple, physical tasks. He never fully recovered from his broken ankle, and had an increasingly difficult time walking.

Most of the churches Hank started were planted during the years when his physical condition was steadily deteriorating.

It has been a long and difficult road. For the past two years, Hank has been in a wheelchair, is unable to drive and needs personal assistance for several hours a day. Some days are better than others for Hank; some days he cannot even get out of bed. But Hank still carries on with the churches, and they continue to view him as their spiritual leader. Because of his condition, he has been developing other leaders who now take responsibility for the churches. Members of the network of churches often visit him at home and look after him. Frequently, the churches meet in his apartment around his wheelchair.

You might think Hank would have given in to discouragement by now. But Hank is unfailingly cheerful and always ready to get excited about what his Lord is doing. His faith continues to grow, because these days he has to rely on God even more.

Pray for Hank!

KEY THOUGHTS: GOD USES ORDINARY PEOPLE TO DO THE EXTRAORDINARY

All over the world, God is using ordinary believers like Hank— or you and me—to plant churches. In some countries, such as China, India and many others, hundreds of thousands of people become Christians every year because of the multiplication of these simpler forms of church. In the Western world, indications are that God is close to doing something similar.

It no longer is up to the trained professional who has been to Bible College or seminary to advance the Kingdom. Housewives and factory workers, businessmen and doctors are leaving the comfort of the pew and heading into their world to make disciples and gather them into small groups called house, organic or simple churches.

Many non-Christians will not darken the door of a church building. Just imagine what would happen if all over this country, ordinary men and women by the thousands were equipped and then released to make disciples and start churches in the homes of these people.

About one third of Christians in this country are outside the organized church, but they have not given up on their Lord, They also have many unbelievers in their circle of friends. What could happen if they also caught hold of this vision?

God will use anyone who is willing to advance His Kingdom. The question is, are we ready to let God use us?

When I look at Hank, I know I have no excuse!

TONY & FELICITY'S STORY

What is church?

WE ARE MOVING TO AMERICA!

"Has the Lord been saying anything to you on this trip?"

My husband, Tony, and I were 35,000 feet above the Atlantic Ocean, flying back home to England. We had been speaking at various churches in California.

"Yes," I replied. "I sensed Him speaking to me about our future. How about you?"

"I'm the same way," he answered. "You go first."

"I think the Lord is telling us to move to the States!"

"Wow! That's what He told me, too!"

This was not the first time the Lord had used this method to speak to us.

"I've been thinking about CiCP," Tony added. "There's just one person I have in mind to take over leadership of it, and that's Derek. Maybe the Lord wants us to hand over leadership in the U.K. to him, and then we could move to the States to start it there."

"Derek's such a busy doctor," I commented. "How would he possibly have time to take on those extra responsibilities?"

"Christians in the Caring Professions" is a ministry Tony led for many years in England. Its purpose is to help doctors, nurses and others in the medical field bring their faith into their professional lives. It focuses on teaching them how to lead their patients to the Lord, or how to pray with them for healing or deliverance—all within the context of the doctor's office. Over the years, God greatly blessed this ministry. Thousands of doctors and others with similar callings attended the conferences that we ran each year in England and in several other countries. Tony was working full time in that ministry

11

when we sensed the Lord speaking to us.

We had been home for less than 24 hours when Tony received a phone call from Derek.

"I was in church yesterday morning," he said, "and someone prophesied over me that I have a major change coming in my life. The more I've thought and prayed over it, the more I have sensed I should be in contact with you. Do you have any idea what this might mean?"

Five months later, Tony and I, our four young children and 12 of the biggest boxes the airline would allow arrived in Texas.

It was a good thing the Lord led us as clearly as He did to move from England to the States; because having dumped us in Texas, He returned back to England. And He did not show up in our lives again for nine, very long, very painful years.

It was not that we didn't like living in the States—we loved it! We loved the people, the country and the food...What we couldn't handle was the absence of God's presence. You see, in England, although we didn't realize it at the time, we were involved in a revival—a church planting movement. From the late 1960s on, spontaneously all over the country, churches emerged at a grass-roots level. They started in homes, which spawned the name, "the British house church movement." But as the churches grew, they moved into buildings. They were characterized by deep fellowship, by "non-religious Christianity" (a Christianity not based on rules and regulations, but motivated by the life of the Spirit within) and by team leadership. In the churches we were involved in, one of the key values was the priesthood of all believers, where everyone participates.

During the movement in England, initially we were involved in starting a church at the hospital where we both were trained as physicians. That church then sent us out into a very poor area of London, where we started another church. Much of the growth of that church was due to patients finding the Lord. And, like most of the other house churches across the nation, it quickly grew to become one of the largest churches in the area.

CiCP also experienced a remarkable working of the Holy Spirit, touching thousands of doctors, and through them, their patients. For example, there were many Christian doctors involved with us in our area of London, at that time a very socially deprived community of around 150,000 people. One day we did the math and calculated that any person getting sick in our area stood a one-in-three chance of sitting down with a Christian doctor who was looking for an opportunity to share the Lord with his patients.

So when we landed in the States, we moved from a place of outstanding blessing and influence into a spiritual desert. Over our first nine years here, we participated in several very good, traditional churches, but we just did not fit in. The Christianity we had known was so different, and we made so many mistakes. It was as though the Lord was giving us a crash course in American church life. He also took the opportunity to deal with our character!

Not only did we fail to integrate into the church, but everything we thought God wanted to accomplish through us in the States resulted in nothing. CiCP went over like a lead balloon—only the Holy Spirit could have shut the doors as firmly as He did. And no one wanted to employ an unlicensed physician. (It would have taken four to five years to get our American medical licenses.)

I would like to tell you that I handled this situation with grace and dignity. I did not. To start with, I repented of everything—real or imaginary—that I could think of. Then I begged the Lord to show us where we were sinning. Finally, I complained. I whined. I wept. I shouted at Him. But to no avail. The heavens remained like brass for a long, long time.

We finally arrived at the point where we gave the Lord a deadline. Either things changed, or we were on our way back to England, where at least we could earn a decent living!

IT'S OK TO START A CHURCH

Slowly things started to change.

The most important shift was that God started communicating with us again.

"You will have the privilege of being part of a move of My Spirit again," was one of the first things He told us. Wow! Was God about to do something amazing in North America?

To try to increase our income, we started a business when we first moved here. It was fairly successful, and we had a considerable number of business associates, many of whom were unbelievers. In fact, for the first time in many years, the majority of our friends did not know the Lord. Tony had the idea of pulling a group of our business leaders together to see if we could introduce some spiritual concepts into the mix.

"Come on Friday evening for pizza. We're going to look at business principles and how to handle wealth. We'll be using a book for our discussions written by a man who is supposed to be the wisest person who ever lived," he told them.

So every Friday evening for a year, a group of about 12 of us came together. We ate pizza, and we discussed the book of Proverbs in an interactive way. There was one rule for our discussions: No rules. Everyone's opinion mattered. There were no wrong answers. But if the Bible had anything to say about whatever we were discussing, that would be our authority on the subject.

The discussions were lively and wide ranging. It did not take long before the Bible was accepted as the final word on any subject. The seed of the Kingdom truly is the Word of God (Mark 4:14), and it didn't take long before that seed started to bear fruit. I recall one wonderful evening when two members of the group, both ex-drug dealers, were quite seriously discussing why some of their drug deals hadn't worked.

"We weren't following the principles in Proverbs!" they agreed. Tony and I were struggling not to laugh that such an exchange was even possible.

Over the course of that year, each person in the group gave their life to Jesus!

At that stage, we were going to a good church that met in a hotel about 30 minutes away from our home. They were doing a great job of incorporating our new believers into what was going on there. But when they physically moved to a building 20 minutes further away, we decided we had to do something different. So we spoke with the senior pastor.

"Why don't you start your own church?" he suggested. "You've done it before in England. The statistics show that the best means of evangelism is to start a church."

We had always resisted that idea before, but his logic was undeniable.

At the time, we had four teenagers, with the two youngest living at home. What would we do about them?

We decided to start what we called a "Breakfast Bible Club." Our kids invited all their friends from our neighborhood.

"Tell them that we will cook a huge breakfast for them!"

We settled on having the club on Sunday morning. We wanted to reach the non-Christian kids, and we figured that the kids from Christian families would be in church on Sunday mornings. It didn't take long for word to get around our neighborhood, and we soon found our house full of kids every Sunday morning. Their parents were delighted because it allowed them to sleep in. The kids came for the food, but they stayed for the activities, which again were interactive and based on the Bible. And they, too, started to become Christians. Soon there were 15 or more who had given their lives over to God. Eventually some of them brought their families, who wanted to know why their kids' lives were changing.

Eventually we merged the group of business people and the kids' group, and wound up with 50-plus people in our living room, hallway, kitchen and dining area, up the stairs and in every conceivable space. We ate together, spent time in worship and sharing, and then divided into small groups to study the Bible. One of the families from across the street got involved, and they also opened up their home so that we could divide into multiple smaller groups whenever needed. We prayed for one another, and God answered. Occasionally, we would see miracles happen.

One Sunday morning, a word of knowledge was given that someone there was about to have a life-threatening condition. (A "word of knowledge" occurs when God supernaturally gives a piece of information no one would naturally know.) Of course we were all very concerned, and someone prayed specifically over John, one of the guys in the church.

During the course of that week, John started to bleed from one of his eyes. When he went to the doctor, tests showed a tumor behind one of his eyeballs.

The following Sunday, several in the group prayed for John to be healed. He was due back at the hospital the next day for a biopsy. But when doctors repeated the tests to find the exact location of the tumor so they could take the biopsy, the tumor was gone. God had healed him!

Our times of meeting together were precious. They were based on I Corinthians 14:26, which states that every person has a valuable contribution to make within the church. The kids were no exception. The Holy Spirit would often speak most clearly through them. Our times together were never boring.

"What are we going to do?" I asked Tony one day. "We've outgrown our house now."

During our nine years of "wilderness," we often discussed the fact that the most meaningful times we had in England were in the early days when the churches we started were still small. It seemed so much easier to obey the New Testament in a small-group context. How could you bear one another's burdens, or teach and admonish one another, if there were 100, or even 50 of you? Not only that, we knew that in countries such as China, the church was expanding very rapidly by multiplying small churches.

"Well, we could rent a building and get larger," Tony replied. "Or we could try to multiply smaller churches meeting in homes or wherever people live life."

"What is a church anyway?" I inquired. "Suppose a church really is what it talks about in Matthew 18, that when two or three are gathered together in His name, Jesus is there in the midst of them. If that is real church, then anyone can start one."

"And the New Testament passages that talk about how you behave toward one another would make sense," Tony added. "You really can only do that in the context of a small group."

This was a major paradigm shift in our thinking, but it did seem to be what the Scriptures offered.

So we made the first of many mistakes in our experience with simple churches. We split the group down the middle. For about a year, people would come to us complaining that it felt like they had been through a divorce. You see, relationships were so deep and meaningful within the group, we really were like family. (Nowadays, when we get too large, we prefer to birth a daughter church

16

where one or two from the parent church will help create a church in the home of someone new.)

Over the next year or so, we grew to three churches. At this rate, it would take us forever to make an impact on our community!

LEARNING FROM OTHER NATIONS

We were watching the news one day in February of 2000, when reports came in about devastating floods in the country of Mozambique, a nation in the southern part of Africa. Half of the country was under water.

"That's where Rolland and Heidi Baker are!" Tony exclaimed. "I wonder if there's anything I can do to help." Rolland was a good friend of Tony's—they had grown up together on the mission field and attended the same boarding school.

Less than two weeks later, Tony and Kathy, a friend of ours who is a nurse, flew to Mozambique. In the two weeks leading up to the trip, we collected money and purchased tens of thousands of dollars worth of medicines.

Rolland and Heidi were asked to take responsibility for some of the refugee camps for those displaced by the floods. Whenever they went to one of the camps, they preached the gospel, and God started to move in power. Hundreds, and then thousands, of people in the camps gave their lives to the Lord.

Tony and Kathy were based out of the orphanage built by Rolland and Heidi. But every day, the United Nations flew them by helicopter to a different refugee camp located on higher ground. They often were the first-ever medical people in the area. They took supplies of food and blankets and Bibles. Sometimes there was a mini-stampede for these items. But often the people were more interested in the boxes of Bibles than in the food!

The people of Mozambique are desperately poor. They live in small reed huts with mud floors. They have no furniture, no electricity or running water, and frequently they wear the only clothing they possess.

Tony and Kathy set up clinics under a tree, or in an old army tent or building. People emerged, seemingly from nowhere out of the bush, to be seen by the doctor. Several times during the day, Tony and Kathy stopped their medical work and preached through an interpreter.

"Some of you are sick because germs that you cannot see are affecting your bodies," Tony told the group. "Even though you cannot see sin, it's like the germs that are making you sick. Sin is choosing to live life your own way rather than the way God, your Creator, wants you to live. That sin causes spiritual death in your life. But God loves you so much that He sent His Son, Jesus, to die for you on a cross, and He took this death for you. If you will surrender your life to Him, He will take away your sin and you can have a new life. If any of you would like to give your life to Him, raise your hand."

Everyone raised their hands.

"No, no! You don't understand. This means giving up your witch doctors and your other gods. You need to give your life totally to Jesus alone. Who still wants to give their lives to Him?"

Again, everyone raised their hands. Tony prayed for them, and the people rejoiced as only they can in Africa—with singing and dancing. By the time Tony and Kathy left after a day or so, there were often 100 or more new believers. Rolland and Heidi sent in pastors trained at the orphanage to help the new church.

Every day or so, Tony sent home an email to report what was happening. There was considerable interest in his emails—which were widely distributed—and our local newspaper did a two-page spread on the events in Mozambique. After hearing about the need for clothing for so many that lost everything they possessed, the house churches started a collection for the people in Mozambique, and the idea quickly caught on. Soon we were receiving bundles of used clothes from various traditional churches and schools around the city. We eventually sent a 40-foot container crammed full of clothing for distribution.

When Tony and I and two of our kids went to Mozambique three months later to continue the medical relief work, we saw a wonderful example of how some of the clothes were used. We were camped (literally) in a village square with a flagpole in the center. (This village seemed to be the center of rooster activity for the region—a chorus started up in full cry around 2:00 A.M. every morning just outside our tents. Maybe they were retaliating because we feasted on one their friends!) Every morning while we were having breakfast, a man dressed in rags with flip-flops on his feet marched up to the flagpole to raise the Mozambican flag—a ceremony conducted with great solemnity. However, one morning it was raining. The rain didn't deter him, but he wore a bright pink lady's fashion coat over his rags to keep out the rain!

It was a life-changing experience for us to be in the center of the revival there. That revival with Rolland and Heidi has continued and more than 6,000 churches have been established in Mozambique and the surrounding nations. Amazing miracles and healings are occurring: The blind see, the deaf hear and even the dead have been raised to life! In Mozambique, it was not church in a building or in a house. It usually was church under the tree! But it was more church in the real sense than is normally known in the most ornate cathedral.

A few months later, we had the privilege of seeing another church planting movement—this time in India. We were invited there by someone who ran across our names on the Internet; for some reason, we felt led to go.

India is an amazing country. There are people everywhere! The traffic has to be experienced to be believed. We came to the conclusion that there is only one rule on the roads: The larger vehicle wins—unless of course, there is a cow involved. Every driver keeps his hand jammed down on the horn. It was our first time to see six people riding on one motor bike. It was also our first taste of severe urban poverty. Chennai (Madras), the city we flew into, has a population of 10 million. Of those, one million live on the streets, (literally sleeping on the sidewalk) and four million more live in slums—often just a sheet of plastic or cardboard leaning against a wall. It was somehow a much more degrading poverty than the rural poverty of Mozambique.

The people may have been poor materially. But at a spiritual level, the Christians put us to shame! I remember meeting a team of five girls, between 15 and 19 years old, who evangelized in the villages every weekend. They certainly faced ridicule, but they also stood a chance of being beaten up and thrown out of the village. Christians in India are often physically persecuted, even to the extent of broken bones. And in the U.S., I was too scared to talk to someone about the Lord in a grocery line!

We were challenged by a number of things we saw and heard. We heard about a middle-aged housewife who started 50 churches in one year. We learned of an elderly gentleman who in the first year following his conversion started 42 churches. Were we just playing at church back at home?

Another major paradigm in our thinking shifted.

"The resources for church planting are in the harvest. This means that new church leaders and planters are probably not even Christians yet."

We were supposed to be teaching these people how to start churches in their homes. But we were the ones who were really learning, and He was using our own teaching to instruct us! We were also amazed when these Indian Christians believed what we told them. We received several emails shortly after we arrived home that said things such as, "Please pray for me. I have started five churches since you were here."

How were we supposed to respond to this? I started to pray.

"Lord, I don't have the faith to start 50 churches in a year, but maybe I could have the faith for our little network of churches to grow to 10."

What would God do in response to such a prayer?

MORE RAPID GROWTH

Around this time, Tony's mother approached me. A retired missionary from China, Taiwan and Hong Kong, she lived in a retirement community after Tony's father died and had started a Bible study for the residents there.

"Would you be willing to take over my Bible study for me? I'm writing a book and just don't have the time to commit to it any longer."

The last thing I planned was running a Bible study in a retirement center. But Tony's mother is a very persistent lady, and it wasn't long before I said I would try it.

After my first week there, I was sold. The old ladies were delightful. Some of them knew the Lord, while others were more nominal Christians. We shared what was going on in people's lives, studied the Bible and prayed.

"You know, Tony," I said to him after a couple of weeks. "I think this is church. These people live more like the New Testament than any other church I know. They are literally sharing their lives together on a daily basis. They eat their meals together, and they have far more community than most churches. What do you think?"

"If our definition of church is 'where two or three gather in His name,' then it definitely is church."

"If that really is church, then we could see if any of the other local retirement communities are interested."

A few days later, I went to a new retirement home just down the road from us.

"Would you be interested in having a Bible study for the residents here?" I asked. (I did not use the word "church" in case that caused a problem for the management.)

"Why yes! The old people would love that. When can you start?"

It was that simple. Not only did they provide a room, they also announced the meeting over the public address system, and the staff made sure that residents who were interested made it to the meeting. After a few weeks, I handed over leadership to an 86-year-old lady from the first retirement center. She ran it until ill health caused her to stop.

We saw other groups start in offices, neighborhoods, apartment complexes and low-income housing projects. One began amongst a group of Catholics; they still attended Mass on the weekends, but "real church" for them was their group that met on a Wednesday night.

Our daughter, Becky, was a vivacious teen and has always been a natural evangelist. She wanted to graduate from high school early in order to spend a year with YWAM. (Youth with a Mission is a Christian missions organization that trains primarily youth, and sends them all over the world into mission situations.) The Christian school she attended most of her life would not allow the early graduation. So she transferred to our local public school, where she made many non-Christian friends.

A few months before she was due to leave for YWAM, Becky decided she wanted to do something to reach these friends. This was precipitated by a friend of hers attempting suicide. When a group of them went to visit her in the hospital, Becky discovered that of the 10 girls present, only she and one other girl (also from a Christian family) had never tried to kill themselves! So she pulled a group of them together to meet at our home for pizza or a barbecue and to discuss spirituality. Each week, we asked one of them to talk about their spiritual journey.

The first week, Helen agreed to share her story. She told how she had been living with her mother in a different state. But following a massive argument, she was shipped off to live with her father and step-mother in Texas. She went from being a cheerleader, knowing everyone and doing well in school, to knowing no one and struggling academically because so many of her credits didn't transfer. During the first few months after the move, she became more and more depressed.

"One day I found myself in the bathroom," she related. "I had all the pills out of the medicine cabinet lined up in front of me and I was about to take them all. But before I did, I cried out, 'God, if there is a God, will you help me?' All of a sudden, I found myself face down on the floor, and God met me there. Within a couple of days, I met Becky. That was just a few weeks ago."

The group's reaction was very interesting. It was a group of about 14 kids, and all of us—even the cool teenage guys—had tears running down our cheeks. It was easy to talk about Jesus in such a context.

Each week, a different one told their story and we spent time studying the Bible together and praying for each other. The kids soon treated our home as their home. We never knew who we would find sleeping on our couch when we woke in the morning!

The night before Becky left for YWAM, we held a going-away party for her.

"I want to tell more of my friends about Jesus," she said. She decided to get baptized again as a sign of recommitting her life to the Lord. That evening, 50 of her "closest friends" came. They listened as she told the story of God's work in her life, and watched as she was baptized in our hot tub.

Even after Becky moved away, the kids continued to meet at our home. We often played crazy games like Pictionary with them until late into the night. And they started to give their lives to the Lord. We usually could tell because they began to clean up their lives. They stopped drinking and partying every night; eventually they asked if they could get baptized. We did not push them into "praying the sinner's prayer" or "making a decision." But when they asked about baptism, we made sure they understood and had committed their lives to the Lord. Our Jacuzzi became the regular place for these baptisms.

For these kids, belonging to the group was very important—even before they believed in Jesus. This was a new concept for us. When we were young, we believed first, and then joined a church. But these kids belonged first, and entered the discipleship process. Their lives changed, and somewhere in the process, they recognized that they believed in Jesus. We have seen this happen many times since then.

After a few months, we decided it was time the kids took responsibility for their meetings.

"We could have it at my home," offered Troy, one of the first to commit his life to the Lord. He had recently moved into a house with three other Christians from one of the local churches.

The first night the group met in his home, a whole new group of people showed up.

"I want to learn more about God and giving my life to Him!" announced Katy, one of the newcomers, as she walked in through the door. She gave her life to Jesus that night, and her boyfriend followed a few weeks later. The meeting grew in size, and quickly two other groups started from it. But we did not foresee some problems.

We returned home after a few weeks on a mission trip, and Troy told us, "I had to shut down the church."

"Why? What happened?" we asked, dismayed.

"The youth pastor from the church that my roommates attend heard about what we were doing. He came along, and thought someone should be doing some teaching. Basically, he took over the whole thing and started running it himself. I didn't know what to do about it, and people didn't want to come any more, so I stopped it."

More lessons for us to learn!

When Becky came back from YWAM, she sensed the Lord wanted her to work downtown in our bar district, so she applied for a job working in a bar. We were hesitant to begin with. Would she be safe? What would our Christian friends think?

Jesus was accused of being a "glutton and a drunkard, and a friend of the worst sort of sinners!" (Matt 11:19) We decided that if hanging out in bars would not have been a problem for Him, we would see what the Lord would do through Becky.

The following Christmas, after Becky had been working as a cocktail waitress for a few months, she asked if she could have a barbecue at our home for her new friends. She invited them to a "Baby Jesus Barbecue." (I must admit, I wondered what people thought we would eat!) That evening, about 40 bartenders and bouncers were in our home. We began a church with them, too. Although the church did not last, several of them became Christians.

LESSONS AND CHALLENGES

We weren't able to help Troy because we were away on another mission trip to India—this time speaking in a number of different states. We had the huge privilege of sharing the platform at one of the conferences with an Indian doctor God has used to spark a church planting movement across his part of the nation. In 1992, the Lord instructed him to leave his position as head of a prestigious medical center, and plant churches instead. He had no idea how to do this, and studied the only materials he knew covering the subject—the Gospels and the Book of Acts. We made sure he was the one who spoke most of the time, while we took copious notes. At every break we deluged him with questions. This humble man of God graciously answered us, and we learned much from him.

"What is a church?" we asked him.

"A church is where two or three meet in Jesus' name," he told us. "But when we used that definition to count the number of churches that started, the numbers seemed artificially high. We decided that since the Bible only counted heads of households, we would only count churches with two or three families in them. Then we added other criteria. The "two or three" must be baptized. (In this particular Indian state, both the person getting baptized and the one doing the baptizing face a three-year jail sentence.) The church has to be led by someone from that village, not an outsider. And finally, we decided that since churches are supposed to multiply, we would only count them in our numbers if they also birthed another church. Nothing living that God created is supposed to be sterile, and that includes the church!"

"How many churches do you have now?" we asked him.

"In the past four years, we have seen about 3,500 started," he replied. "Of course, there are thousands more 'triplet churches,' where two or three are gathered in His name."

Back at home, we were still adding churches. We had a monthly celebration on a Sunday morning to draw all the churches together. There was a worship team at the celebration, just as in traditional churches, and someone taught. There was a full program for the kids. But the celebration ran into some problems.

First, we discovered that our youth—the teens and twenty-somethings who recently had become Christians—did not do mornings! Added to that, some of the families who had recently become believers hadn't cleaned up their language; the four-letter words used by their kids in everyday speech caused problems for the "nice middle-class" Christian families who wanted to protect their own kids from that kind of language.

The leadership team (consisting of four couples) sought the Lord and sensed we should stop the regular monthly celebration. We decided to bring the churches together only if a speaker came to town we wanted everyone to have a chance to hear.

"We are modeling traditional church in our celebrations," we concluded. "Let's see what happens if we reduce the number of times we all get together."

We didn't anticipate the effects this move would produce. Quite a number of Christians who had transferred into the network from other churches left to go back to more traditional models of church. In their minds, the monthly celebration was "real" church and the meetings in homes were just an added extra. They wanted Sunday school for their kids and youth programs for their teens. They might have been out of the traditional church for a while, but the traditional "system" was not out of them.

So the number of churches in our network declined. We were back to working primarily with those who became Christians within the house church context, plus reaching out to unbelievers.

It took a while, but our network of churches has started to grow again. In our city, there are others with a vision of multiplying networks of churches, and they have grown even faster than we have. It is exciting to watch what God is doing.

KEY THOUGHTS: WHAT IS CHURCH?

When Jesus walked on earth, the main theme of His teaching was the Kingdom of God. (Matthew 4:23) Many of His parables illustrated the Kingdom of God (e.g. Matthew 13). Jesus told His disciples to heal people and tell them, "The Kingdom of heaven has come near to you." (Luke 10:9) After His resurrection and before His ascension, He spent forty days talking to his disciples about the Kingdom. (Acts 1:3)

How interesting that, having spent three years living with Jesus on a daily basis, the disciples lived out what they learned from Him about the Kingdom by meeting together in each others' homes on a daily basis and sharing their lives together. (Acts 2:42-47) Could this have been what Jesus modeled for them? Of course! And they called it "church." They also met, probably for evangelism, on a daily basis in the Temple until persecution forced them to scatter. From that point on, all the references to church meetings are in a house—apart from one reference to Paul teaching in the hall of Tyrannus, (possibly a school for church planters, since Paul could say that all of Asia heard the gospel). The first time history gives us any indication that the believers met in buildings is in 321 A.D. when the emperor, Constantine, adopted Christianity and followed pagan tradition by building special "temples" for the Christians. It was from this point that a paid, professional, clergy class arose.

For a subject so significant, it is extraordinary that the word "church" is only mentioned twice in the Gospels. The first occurs in Matthew 16 after Peter's great declaration, "You are the Christ, the Son of the Living God." Jesus responds, "On this rock (i.e. this declaration of truth), I will build My church, and the gates of Hades will not prevail against it" (verse 18). This obviously is referring to the church universal, which is made up of all Christians everywhere in the world, down through the ages. He then goes on to say, "I will give you (the church) the keys of the Kingdom of heaven, and whatever you bind on earth will be bound in heaven and whatever you loose on earth will be loosed in heaven."

The second mention of the word church comes two chapters later in Matthew 18. In verses 15-17, Jesus describes what should happen if someone sins against another. First, you confront the person one-on-one. Then you go to the person with one or two witnesses. Finally, if that has no effect, you should tell it to the church. This reference to church has to refer to a small group situation. It would be most inappropriate applied to a mega church or even a large congregation! And the person concerned would most likely leave that church and go to the one down the street. But in a small group, where relationships are deep and relevant, this kind of action would produce results. After all, the purpose of church discipline is to restore the person back to fellowship.

However, it is the verses following these that are the most interesting. Jesus uses the same concepts here as He did with the universal church. He says "Whatever you bind on earth will be bound in heaven, and whatever you loose on earth will be loosed in heaven." Then He adds, "Again I say to you that if two of you agree on earth concerning anything that they ask, it will be done for them by My Father in heaven. For where two or three are gathered together in My name, I am there in the midst of them" (verses 18-20). In the context of church, Jesus says He is present when two or three are gathered in His name. Many people take this verse as the primary definition of church.

Robert Fitts, in his book *Saturation Church Planting*, says:

"When two or three true, born-again believers come together in His name, Jesus is in the midst. Jesus in the midst is church! It is a different experience than Jesus within. We cannot experience Jesus in the midst when we are alone. We can only experience Jesus in the midst when we are in company with others—at least one or two others.

"But is it church in the fullest sense of the word? Yes, it is a church in the fullest sense of the word. It is the basic church. You can have more than two or three and it is still a church, but it does not become "more church" because there are more than two or three. It only becomes bigger church."

Church is mentioned in the New Testament in various other ways. Quite frequently, the term, "church in a house" is used. For example, in Romans 16:5: "Greet the church in their house," refers to the church that met in Priscilla and Aquila's home. This is the outward expression of "where two or three are gathered in My name." The term "church" is also used to describe all of the disciples in a locality, such as a city or region, and was probably made up of many smaller groups. Examples of this would be the church at Antioch (Acts 13:1) or the churches of Galatia. (I Corinthians 16:1)

So we see that in the Scriptures, there are three main uses of the word "church": The church in the home (or the church of at least two or three), the church in a city or region, and the church universal.

However, in our culture, we generally use the word "church" in other ways that are non-Biblical. The most obvious of these is when we refer to a church building, as in, "I left my Bible at church." The term is useful in that everyone knows what we mean, but the church is not a building! The second is when we refer to a denomination, such as the Baptist Church or the Roman Catholic Church. This is more negative in its effects, because the Bible specifically speaks against dividing the body of Christ into different factions. (1 Corinthians 1:10-13) We may also use the term to refer to a specific congregation, such as "New Life Church." Again, this is not a Biblical use of the term.

So what is a church? The word "ekklesia" that is translated "church" literally means "called out ones." It was not exclusively a religious term at all. In fact, elsewhere in the New Testament it is used to describe other kinds of assembly. For example, in Acts 19:32, "ekklesia" is used to refer to a rioting mob.

But is church merely a series of weekly meetings? Even in simple churches, we have a tendency to refer to it this way. No! The church is who we are, 24/7. It is not a place we go or an activity we do. Church as described in the New Testament is something that happens daily. (Acts 2:46) It is more relational than meeting based. We are members of one another. (Ephesians 4:25) Church is about vibrant communities where our common denominator is faith in Christ. Church is a group of disciples relating together in normal life; when they get together in His name, Jesus Himself is present.

There are several different terms being used across the nation to describe what is currently going on. Some refer to these churches as "house churches" or "home churches." Others refer to them as "simple churches" or "organic churches." All these terms refer to a community of God's people who relate together as a small group, loving one another and caring for one another in practical ways. These churches are missional, seeking to multiply by actively reaching into the world of unbelievers or unchurched around them.

(These simple churches are not reaching out to existing Christians in more traditional churches, which we sometimes refer to as "legacy churches." The reason we use the term "legacy churches" is that we value the spiritual deposit that so many of them have given us—truly a great legacy. The last thing we wish for is a group of disgruntled Christians that gets together to complain about the traditional churches they have left. How could God multiply that?)

When we view church through these new lenses, our whole understanding changes.

KENNY'S STORY

The 10:2b virus

A PRAYER MOVEMENT MUST PRECEDE A CHURCH PLANTING MOVEMENT

Kenny does not remember the exact day of his conversion to Christ, but Oct 28, 2002 is a date forever fixed in his mind. On that day, Kenny and his friend, John, were having breakfast together at a local restaurant. As it so often did with them, the conversation quickly turned to their shared passion—church planting, and their desire to see a spontaneous, rapid movement of churches planted across their state.

"How are we ever going to see this state saturated with the gospel?" asked Kenny, as he took a sip of his coffee. "We know it will take a church planting movement."

"The real problem is lack of leadership. The whole idea of a church planting movement hinges on an army of men and women church planters. Workers for the harvest are what we really need," John responded.

"My *modus operandi* has always been to fly out of state and try to enlist a seminary student. If I find someone even half alive, I will suggest, 'Why don't you come to our city and start something?' It's all activity oriented," said Kenny.

"I'm reminded of the passage of Scripture in Luke 10 where Jesus tells his disciples that the harvest is ready, and that we should be praying for workers for the harvest," John added.

"Well I've prayed that prayer in the past when I've been desperate and needed someone to fill in a situation."

"Me too," agreed John.

"But I don't usually keep going. It doesn't take me long before I default to activity. I will pray for a short season, and then I approach someone and say, 'I think God is calling you to do this.' At best, this is just my own effort," confessed Kenny.

"According to that passage, the problem isn't the harvest; it is ripe and ready. The problem is the laborers," said John. "With 72 disciples, there were 36 church planting teams. If you add in the original 12 disciples, that would make 84 total, or 42 teams! Most churches would be thrilled with that number, but Jesus said it was not enough!"

"What do you suggest we do about it?"

"You know, I think there is something more to this command of Jesus in Luke 10:2 than we realize. And this conversation is more than just our normal complaining about the lack of church leaders. God may be doing something here. Why don't we take the next week and pray about it and see what the Lord is trying to tell us? Then let's get back together and compare notes."

The next week, John and Kenny met again for breakfast.

"You know, as I thought and prayed about it this past week, I had this sense that we need to get together to pray regularly for workers for the harvest," John shared.

"I had that same impression," said Kenny. "Do you think we could do it daily?"

"Well, we can't eat breakfast together daily, that's for sure. We're both much too busy."

"What if we do it over the phone?"

"OK, let's try it for a week. If we have the chance to meet together, we'll do it. Otherwise, let's call each other."

Kenny left that meeting with John somewhat uncomfortable with what he was getting himself into.

"This sounds legalistic," he thought to himself. "I'm really not interested in some kind of formula."

But he had agreed with John; so early the next morning, he called John on the phone.

"Hi John, are you ready to pray?"

"Yes, I'm ready."

"Well, Lord. John and I are here to pray together for workers for the harvest. You tell us that the harvest is ready. We cry out to you for laborers for the harvest here in this city. Send us laborers, Lord!"

"And Lord," John continued, "we really don't know how to pray this prayer. Please, will you teach us?"

All went well for a couple of days. But then came the day when they did not connect. When they finally re-established contact, they decided that if they didn't get through to the other person, they would at least leave a voicemail prayer. It sounded a bit bogus, but it was the only thing they could think of.

At the end of the first week, John and Kenny evaluated what was happening.

"We're enjoying it. Let's just keep doing it and see where it goes."

Rather than their daily prayer becoming ritualistic, Kenny looked forward to it. They usually would not pray long, just a few minutes. But the conversation might go longer. They shared briefly about their day so they could pray about that, and they caught up with one another's news. But the focus was on praying for workers for the harvest.

One day led to another, and then one week to another. It now has been more than two years, and Kenny and John have prayed together virtually every day (at the time of writing, they estimate more than 700 times!)

EFFECTIVE PRAYER

As John and Kenny began praying, they quickly realized that they didn't really know how to pray consistently long term. How many times can you pray, "Lord, send out workers into your harvest?" Can it become "vain repetition?"

"How do we do this, Lord?" they asked.

"There were two passages that the Lord seemed to impress on us," says Kenny. "The first, from Luke 18, was the story of an un-righteous judge and a widow woman seeking justice. The widow kept coming back over a long period of time asking the judge for justice. The judge's final response was, 'I don't fear God or man, but this woman has worn me out!' So he gave in to her request. Jesus said this is the way we're supposed to pray. That encouraged us to be persistent and relentless in our praying.

"Sometimes we would tell Him, 'Well, Lord, here we are again, and we're asking you again for church planters for the harvest.'

"Another thing we learned is we need to be more specific in what we ask, and not make a general request. The Greek word for "send" in Luke 10:2 is "ekballo." The word has an element of violence, of a force that a person cannot resist. It's the same word that is used for casting out a demon! "Thrust out" or "throw out" might be more accurate translations. It implies people who are very willing to go. We asked the Lord for people who are already passionate for church planting and have apostolic hearts. God seemed to answer that kind of prayer. The idea of specificity came from a story Jesus tells in Luke chapter 11 about a man who asks his neighbor for bread because he has an unexpected visitor and no food to offer him. But he not only asks for bread; he asks for three loaves of bread. That encourages us to be specific in what we ask Him for."

One day, Kenny thought he would look up Luke 10:2b in a Greek New Testament. He assumed that the command, "Pray the Lord of the harvest," would be a command in the present continuous tense; i.e., one was supposed to pray and keep on praying. To his surprise, he found it is in a tense that implies a one-time action. He called John.

"John, this is a bit disconcerting. Does it mean that we are only supposed to pray once and then believe that God has answered? That would mean the end of our daily praying!"

John went onto the Internet, and the results were interesting. According to his best research, the tense (an aorist imperative) means that at a point in time, you start doing something you haven't been doing and you never quit. Their confidence increased, knowing that it must be in the heart of God to answer that kind of prayer.

Kenny and John quickly saw the results of their praying. In 2002, Kenny was working for the city association of a mainline denomination. (He now coordinates church planting for that denomination in his state.) Almost immediately, he began getting phone calls, emails or visits to his office from people who wanted to start churches in his city. Some of the people were from out of state but planning to move there. Others were people he'd known for 10 or more years from his city but hadn't seen for some time. All said much the same thing.

"I think God is calling me to be involved in church planting."

This got Kenny's attention. Meanwhile, John had similar experiences. However as God answered their prayer, their stereotype and template of a church planter had to change.

"I used to look for a young, energetic, good-looking, educated, charismatic personality to be a church planter," admits Kenny. "We prayed, 'Lord, help us to recognize these people as they emerge.' Now I see a much broader spectrum of ordinary people God might be calling out for this.

"The results of our praying were cool in terms of new church planters," Kenny continues. "But what really happened, as I look back, were the changes that went on in me. If I'm really honest, I never used to believe I was going to get an answer when I prayed. The Lord saved me when I was 30 and I've been a believer almost 35 years. During that time I've prayed a lot, and the Lord has answered many prayers. But I have never before had that sense of expectancy that comes with a real belief in prayer. Prayer used to be a side issue. Now it has become the focus of my strategy for church planting in this state. I do not have a "Plan B." Everything focuses on praying and letting God provide the workers for the harvest.

"Another by-product has been the effect on me spiritually. I'm more passionate about prayer than I've ever been. I've seen my personal prayer life take on a new vitality. And I seem to have more hunger for the Word. My wife complains that all I think about these days is church planting. I tell her, 'I really believe I'm more of a missionary now than I've ever been in my life.' That's hard to quantify, but I find that I have more burden for the lost, and more interest in the harvest than I've had in 20 years."

THE VIRUS REPLICATES

"Wouldn't it be amazing if this thing spread out to others?" John suggested one day. "It would be like a virus! People could catch the virus and then infect others with it. I'll tell you what, let's call it the 10:2b virus since it's in the second part of Luke 10:2."

"How do we get other people to join us in our praying? We can't do it by giving away books or creating a program. I think all we can do is tell our story!"

With that in mind, John and Kenny have committed to each other that they will take the opportunity to tell their story wherever they go. If they have lunch with someone, they share the virus with them. If they are speaking at a meeting, they talk about it. And it has grown into at least a mini-movement. All around their state, and indeed across the country, people are calling each other daily on the phone and praying the 10:2b virus: "Lord, send out laborers into Your harvest." A couple of groups even get together monthly to pray and share the stories of answered prayer.

As Kenny and John continue to pray for harvesters, they are also praying that a prayer movement will permeate their state. They believe if this happens a church planting movement will result. They have concluded they never will see a true church planting movement unless it is preceded by a prayer movement.

Their prayer together usually takes only a few minutes.

"If it lasts any longer than that, it will be harder to sustain," says Kenny. "A typical prayer goes something like this. 'Lord, we're here again today to thank you for answered prayer in sending harvesters. Thank you for Andrew who contacted me yesterday and who is coming back to this state, interested in church planting. But we're also here today to ask you for more! Give us an army of men and women who are prepared and who don't need a lot of training. Let them have the passion and burden to be involved in church planting and gospel saturation in this state. Lord, we pray for each of the counties in this state. Give us a team of two people who are willing to pray daily for the people in their county.

"'Father, I also pray for John's meeting today with George. Give John wisdom as he mentors him. Use John to encourage him and give him any insights he might need. Bless John today in Jesus' name. Amen.'

"We try to keep the prayer primarily focused on the harvest. In the denomination I serve, prayer meetings usually focus on sick bodies and sad circumstances. 'So and so is sick and needs our prayer,' or 'My husband has lost his job.' But we try to keep our prayer focused on the Kingdom."

The effects of praying the virus are beginning to show.

A VIRAL EPIDEMIC

Many stories are emerging about churches that have started as a result of these prayers.

Just before the National House Church conference put on by House2House Ministries in 2003, a young man came to Kenny's office. Kenny had known Tim, who worked as a pastor in a traditional church, for a number of years.

"I'm leaving my church," he said. "I really believe that the Lord is calling me to start a house church and a network of house churches."

He and Kenny talked for a minute. Tim obviously had a good understanding of the concepts of simple church from books he had read on the subject. But he had never been in one.

"You need to go to the House2House conference and look up my friend John. Say to him, 'My name is Tim, and I'm an answer to Luke 10:2b.'"

Tim followed Kenny's instructions, much to John's surprise and delight! Tim came back from the conference and started planting house churches! He now has seven or eight churches in his network. He took a few folks from the traditional church and has reached out to unchurched Christians. A lot of people from elsewhere have heard about what he is doing and have plugged in. As yet, though, they have not seen much growth through conversion.

That is not true of some of the other networks that have started.

A colleague of Kenny's, who also works for the denomination, has a heart for house churches. Kenny and his language coordinator, Lorenzo, have mentored Otto, a German guy in his sixties who grew up in Argentina. Otto came to their state a couple of years ago, at that stage very traditional in his thinking. But now he works in a rural area, in a farming community. He is reaching out to migrant workers, and has started 10 churches, all by conversion growth. He is leading some of them himself, and he is working hard to develop leaders.

A cabinet installer has started another network. He is reaching out to blue-collar workers and people in the construction industry. He is also involved in the biking community, and is engaging with some people that many would feel extremely nervous about turning loose in the church! But these people are reaching out to the bikers, to the unchurched and the never-churched; many lives are being transformed.

A seminary professor is leading another network. He started a church in his home which has now expanded to five or six churches reaching a wide variety of people. One person in his network is reaching out to the urban core of their city, especially to the Goth community. Other churches are reaching out to their neighborhoods with an emphasis on working with kids. Many of the leaders in this network are women.

"I've been trying to get something started with Muslims," Kenny mentioned to John one day. "Did you know there are 13 mosques in this city? I've made several aborted attempts in the past to make it happen. Can we pray for a team to work with Arabic speaking people?"

For several months, John and Kenny included the Arabic speaking world in their prayers.

Then one day, a Lebanese friend of Kenny's called him.

"Kenny, we've failed in this stuff before, but I think now's the time! And I have a guy who may be the man."

"I'm going to believe that this is God's doing." And Kenny told his friend the story of the 10:2b virus.

A few weeks later, a group of Arabic speaking people came together. It included Iraqis, Somalis, Afghanis, Lebanese and Egyptians. All of them Christians, they came together with the desire to start an Arabic speaking church. The young man who is leading it is obviously very gifted. He has a great grasp of how to strategize to reach a people group. This is an exciting possibility.

In addition to Anglo church planters, John has been thrilled to see the Lord of the harvest send church planters who have a vision for other people groups in the city. Paulo is a Filipino pastor who has helped start three Filipino house churches. Alex is a Russian businessman who has started two Russian-speaking churches. Richard, a former missionary, has started a Japanese church.

Day by day, Kenny receives inquiries from people who want to get involved in church planting. Some are interested in starting simple churches; others want to start a traditional church. Not all of them materialize into church planters. According to Kenny's best estimates, around 100 house churches have started in the last eight months, some of which are in an embryonic phase. Last year, around 20 traditional churches also started. (He does not count churches that have already started.) But whether they are house church or traditional church, all are part of his "tribe" or denomination. Kenny is praying that all types of expressions of church will emerge. He wants to see his state saturated with the gospel.

KEY THOUGHTS: THE 10:2b VIRUS

Kenny and John are seeing a prayer epidemic launched. We all know that prayer is the key to seeing God move in power. If we really believed it, as opposed to merely giving it lip service, would we spend more time on our faces before God?

I recently read an account of an interview with Dr. Paul (David) Yonggi Cho (pastor of the largest church in the world). The interviewer asked his secret. His reply, in effect, was that when he first started, it took four to five hours of prayer a day to see God move, but now he has been able to cut down to three hours per day! If we want to see a true, sustained move of God, we have to be willing to pay a similar price.

A few years ago, the International Mission Board of the Southern Baptist Convention identified a new phenomenon occurring in many parts of the world (with the noticeable exception of here in the West). As they studied reports from their missionaries, they observed a spontaneous and rapid growth in churches started in some areas—often described as "nearly out of control." This rapid growth was due to conversions, not just transfer of Christians from one church to another. They saw a genuine advance for the Kingdom of God. They called what they saw a "church planting movement." They define a church planting movement as "a rapid and multiplicative increase of indigenous churches planting churches within a given people group or population segment." For example, in a little more than a decade in Cambodia, the number of Christians has increased from around 600 to more than 100,000!

This is what we are longing for and praying for here, too. We may not be seeing it yet, but the signs point to God doing something unusual.

The research of the International Mission Board showed several key, common characteristics in the places that experienced outstanding growth. Prayer is one of these.

This movement needs to be birthed and bathed in prayer. I

believe that much of what we are seeing has been initiated by the prayer movement of the last decade or so. But we need people who are willing to spend time on their faces before God, crying out for Him to do something far beyond man's best abilities to produce, something that only He can do (and only He will get the credit for). "Unless the Lord builds the house, those who build it labor in vain." (Psalm 127:1) Where are those who will seek His face, hour after hour, pleading with Him for a move of His Holy Spirit that will transform this nation? Where are those who will pray until all across this land, ordinary disciples are motivated to move out of their comfort zones to preach good news to the poor, comfort the afflicted, and announce freedom to the captives? (Isaiah 61:1)

Am I willing to pay this kind of price? Are you?

John has an e-list of people who are praying the 10:2b Prayer. People on the list share stories of how the Lord of the Harvest has sent out harvest workers into their region or people group. If you would like to be added to that group, email John at DenverWH@aol. com with your name, location and email address. Just ask to be added to the "10:2b List."

ELIZABETH'S STORY

The Great Commission

TRAUMATIC BEGINNINGS

"The moment I step foot outside my door, I'm in a mission field!"

Elizabeth is bold in her witness for the Lord, but it is adversity that has made her so courageous.

The eighth year of Elizabeth's life was marked by two events; she spent several weeks in the hospital with a diagnosis of juvenile diabetes, and her father and mother separated. Most of the time, Elizabeth lived with her mother. But that year for summer break, she stayed with her father. One night he sat her on his lap.

"Elizabeth, you know I've lost contact with my other kids, but I just want you to know that I love you and I'll never leave you." Her father had three children by a former wife, but was no longer in touch with them.

Later that night, her father took an entire bottle of codeine in a suicide attempt. Elizabeth was the one who found him. She called his current girlfriend.

"Help me, I can't wake Dad."

The paramedics were called, and Elizabeth watched in anguish as he was taken in the ambulance. Her father survived. But he was filled with so much guilt and shame, that he never contacted her again.

In her early teens, Elizabeth began partying heavily. She turned to the ways of the world to fill the vacancy left by her absent father. She became promiscuous at a very early age because of her longing to be accepted by any male figure. Her diabetes went out of control because she refused to take care of herself; she was constantly sick and frequently in the hospital.

Elizabeth had three best friends who were there for her throughout her entire ordeal. They frequently visited her in the hospital; and after she came home, they spent all their time together. One particular day, a group of them spent the evening at her mother's home.

"Let's all go get some coffee. Hey, I'll drive," suggested Kylie, her closest friend.

"No, you can't drive my car," Elizabeth said.

"Oh, let me, please let me," Kylie begged. She kept on, until finally Elizabeth threw the keys at her.

"Be careful!" she said.

She climbed into the passenger seat and put on her seat belt.

"Don't come with me. You go with Jason," ordered Kylie. Kylie wanted Elizabeth to get back with Jason, her ex-boyfriend, who was going to be following them in a truck.

Elizabeth switched cars. She climbed into the front seat of the truck and one of the guys took her place in her car.

On the way to the coffee shop there was a horrendous wreck involving Elizabeth's car. Her three best friends were killed instantly, and the other two in the car suffered major trauma. Elizabeth witnessed the whole thing.

This was the darkest day of Elizabeth's life! When she looks back on it now, she wonders how she ever got through. Three vibrant, healthy girls died and she, so sick she often felt there was nothing left to live for, survived.

By the grace of God, Elizabeth picked up the pieces of her life again.

However, maybe as a consequence of the shock, Elizabeth soon developed a peripheral neuropathy, a complication of diabetes that affects the nervous system. In considerable pain, and with her weight down to 72 pounds, she was very seriously ill. She was hospitalized again—this time for 15 months. Although she eventually recovered, she wore leg braces from then on.

Within two years, her diabetes caused serious eye problems that required multiple surgeries. The surgery worsened the condition of her right eye; there was so much scar tissue that the retina eventually detached and she became blind in that eye. But the sight in her left eye was saved, and she has 20/40 vision in that eye. (Overall she has about 70% loss of vision.)

Just before her eyesight deteriorated and she could no longer drive a car, Elizabeth had a job driving for a girl, Laurie, who had become partially sighted also due to diabetes. Longing for another close friend, she and Laurie did all kinds of things together, eventually sharing a condo for several months. Laurie was a believer, and Elizabeth went to church with her a couple of times. Elizabeth had been born and raised Catholic. She didn't really understand nor have any relationship with the Lord. But through this friendship, she began thinking more about Him.

One Christmas, Laurie went to see her grandmother and family in Seattle. Elizabeth never saw her again. Laurie became very sick while she was there, had a cardiac arrest and died at the age of 26. This was another tremendous loss!

By the age of 18, Elizabeth stopped driving because of her eyesight. Life completely changed for her. She was no longer independent. (Elizabeth still thinks she is the most independent person out there. She cannot stand it when people want to help her because she wants to do it on her own!) But God was about to extend a hand into her life.

PHYSICAL AND SPIRITUAL SURGERIES

Shortly after Laurie passed away, Elizabeth went into the hospital again. The doctors didn't know what was wrong, but blood work eventually showed that her kidneys were failing. The specialist told her that if she wanted to survive, she would need to go on dialysis. She required many surgeries and, yet again, her life changed. This time around, she spent three hours a day, three days a week at the dialysis center. She was placed on the waiting list for a kidney transplant.

With all this going on, Elizabeth became hungry for God. She found a rapidly growing mega-church, where an anointed evangelist was the senior pastor, and attended regularly. It did not take long for her to give her life to the Lord, and she matured quickly in her Christian life. For the first time, she had a spiritual family, brothers and sisters who cared about her. Marty, one of the assistant pastors at the church, helped her considerably, and she became strong friends with him and his wife, Vicki. Elizabeth wanted to be involved in everything that was going on. Sometimes she even went to church with a walker because she didn't want to miss out on anything.

More than seven years passed while she waited for a kidney transplant, and her physical condition deteriorated. Finally, doctors told her it would be three more years before she reached the top of the list; but she likely would not live that long. However, if she transferred from the kidney transplant list to the kidney/pancreas transplant list, she would be number one on the list. It would involve more challenges, but at least it would save her life!

Two months later, she had the transplant.

The first year was really tough. There were complications with the new pancreas, and she went back to the operating room three times before it was finally fixed. Recovery eventually took 18 months.

But now, for the first time in 23 years, Elizabeth was off insulin! (The pancreas is the organ that produces insulin.) This freed up her life.

As she started recovering, she became even more active in church. She loved intercessory prayer and worship and always helped wherever she was needed. She had a heart for the lost, and took teams to the local shopping center to minister to the Goths that hung out there. The Lord touched many lives through her life.

But problems surfaced in the church. People started to leave when major moral issues were uncovered. (In fact, seven other churches started from the break-up of this church, two of which are networks of simple churches.) Marty and Vicki, one of the couples who left, were gaining a vision for house churches. They were excited about the possibilities of evangelism within a multi-generational home context.

When Marty and Vicki left the church, they birthed a new church called The River. Very soon, Elizabeth joined them.

Elizabeth's desire one day was to have a home she could open up to the broken and lost. She dreamed of having a church meet in her home.

"When I am married, and there is spiritual leadership in my home, then I will open it up to those in need," she would say.

The River met in another church's building. When Elizabeth went early to prepare for worship, a young man from that church was always there working on the sound system. Scott is a wonderful man, who loves God with all his heart. Many people comment on how much of Jesus they see in him. He and Elizabeth got to know each other and fell in love. Scott even developed a heart to help Elizabeth with her physical disabilities.

One year later they were married.

OBEDIENCE TO THE GREAT COMMISSION

Elizabeth and Scott moved into Scott's home in a mobile home park. One of their first prayers as a married couple was, "Lord, if you want us to open our home to others, please show us how." They knew they needed to be in unity over this decision.

The River was at a point where Marty was focusing the people on outreach to the highways and byways. He wanted to avoid any tendency for the new house churches to get inbred and comfortable. So a few months after their wedding, Scott and Elizabeth found themselves at a house church conference where they heard about simple ways of starting churches with unbelievers. They hung on every word, looking for the Lord to speak.

"Prayer walk in your neighborhood," the speaker shared. "Trust the Lord to bring you to a person of peace."

This was the first time they had heard Luke 10 taught in an intensive manner. The model ignited their hearts.

"We can do this," they thought. They weren't going to wait for Marty to help them or for The River to give them permission to start something. From that point on, they owned the vision. Marty encouraged them to do something about it.

"Let's prayer walk in our neighborhood and see what the Lord opens up," they decided.

A couple of evenings later, Elizabeth bugged Scott.

"You told me we would prayer walk tonight. You have to take me out." She was so determined, Scott eventually gave in.

Elizabeth had a broken foot at the time and could not walk. So Scott put her in a wheel chair and off they went. As they walked around the mobile home park, sometimes they prayed out loud for their neighbors; other times they prayed quietly to themselves. Sometimes the Lord stirred their hearts to pray for things they knew were going on in the various homes.

Scott had lived in the mobile home park for many years and he knew most of the people there by name. He gardened in the park, and often would help people. For many years he prayed and planted the seeds of Christ's love in their lives. People noticed radiance about him. And his prayers would soon produce fruit.

Scott and Elizabeth were nearing their home when someone called out to them.

"Hi, Scott!"

There was a carpet rolled out under the carport of one of the houses, and Janet was relaxing in a chair with a bottle of beer in her hand.

Scott and Elizabeth walked over to her.

"Hi, Janet," they said. "How are you doing?"

"Sit down, sit down! Visit with me." She was excited to see them. "Oh, let me get you a beer. Do you want a beer?"

"Oh, that's OK, Janet. Don't worry."

"Oh no, no, no, I'll get you a beer!"

At that point Scott and Elizabeth remembered the passage in Luke 10, where Jesus told his disciples to eat and drink whatever is set before them.

"Just receive it," they heard the Lord whisper to them.

Elizabeth looked at Scott; they knew this was her way to show hospitality, and they should receive it with a smile!

"Thanks, Janet."

Now let Elizabeth take up the story!

"We received the beer, and what opened up was beautiful. Janet felt comfortable with us because we were meeting her at her level. We weren't playing "holier than thou." We listened to her and loved her. She was a lonely lady who wanted company. She just sat and talked and shared much about her life while we drank half a beer!"

As they were leaving, Elizabeth noticed that Janet had a beautiful vegetable garden. There was an abundance of ripening tomatoes and peppers.

"Oh Janet, your vegetable garden is so neat. I'd really like to have one, too. Maybe you can help me? Would you like to come over for dinner one night?"

"Sure, I can do that."

A few days later, Janet came to dinner, and their friendship began to deepen.

Scott and Elizabeth soon prayed about taking things a step further, and the Lord started to lead them. Sometimes the Lord said to them, "Go and knock on that person's door and say, 'Hello, I'm your neighbor!'" They did that several times. Sometimes as they were walking around the mobile home park, they saw people watering their yards and they would talk with them. They greeted whoever they met at the mailbox. Whenever the opportunity arose, they invited neighbors over for dinner.

Janet helped Elizabeth plant a vegetable garden. Elizabeth planted one plant for every neighbor who came to her home for dinner. She watered the plants and prayed for her neighbors.

"Lord, just as you are making this plant grow, will you help the person this plant represents grow in their relationship with You?"

After a few weeks, Scott and Elizabeth began asking the Lord what should happen next.

"Let's have a neighborhood dinner," Elizabeth suggested one day. "We'll invite all the people that we've had contact with over the last few weeks. And let's see what the Lord does."

When The River heard what they were doing, they gave Scott and Elizabeth one of their "church-in-a-box" kits, consisting of paper plates and cutlery and a dry erase board. Initially, some had qualms about giving the house church tote kit to a couple who was just inviting non-Christians over for dinner.

"Is it really a church if they are not all saved?" was their question.

But Marty's response was clear: "We don't go to church; we *are* the church. If church is where two or three are gathered in His name, then Scott and Elizabeth are enough. They *are* the church. Jesus is going to be there, God will be moving by His Holy Spirit and people are going to be discipled. So what Scott and Elizabeth are doing *is* church."

EATING AND MEETING

When Janet came to the first neighborhood dinner, she brought a friend, Jean (who also has drinking problems). Jean came in clutching a big bottle of red wine, and Janet was carrying a grocery bag containing twelve beers. After the meal, they were sitting in the living room, and Janet spilled one of the beers on the new carpet.

"I'm so sorry, I'm so sorry!" Janet could not apologize enough. Scott ran to get some rags to clean it up.

"I'm so sorry. I know this carpet was new for your wedding!" Janet was really distressed.

"Janet, look at me!" Elizabeth said to her. "I care about you more than I care about this carpet. This carpet can be replaced, but you can't." Janet stared at Elizabeth as if she were an alien.

Janet obviously had never heard such a thing. That is when Janet's life started to change—when she experienced the unconditional love of God through Elizabeth. After that point, she never brought beer to their home.

Elizabeth is bold. She will approach someone and say, "Hey, I'm Liz. We live over there and we're having a neighborhood dinner."

"If I see someone who's broken or hurting, I think to myself, 'Do I go home and pray about this or do we do something about it?' I'm one of those people who like to do something. 'Just go and do it!' We're mistaken if we hear about a need and think all we need to do is pray. We do need to pray—a lot! But God puts a need right in front of us, and all we're going to do is pray about it? Of course not!

"That's why we finally told everyone we'd like to have a neighborhood dinner. The first time, we didn't ask them to bring anything. Many of the people in the mobile home park live on Social Security, and they don't have a lot to offer. What's so neat is that most of the growth occurs around the dining room table. It just happens naturally. We don't say, 'Now let's go into the living room and have a meeting.'

"It's an ongoing process. Janet is a good example. There have been so many changes in her life that I believe she has become a follower of Jesus, even though she may not recognize it yet. She comes from a Jehovah's Witness background. When we first started, Scott and I did all the praying. But now Janet gives thanks for the food. This is a big step for her. She thanks the Lord for good neighbors and that she now has friends who are part of her life.

"At Christmas, the Salvation Army gave Janet a gift basket that contained a turkey meal. She wanted us to have it for our neighborhood meal. We didn't want to take it from her because she has so little. But God spoke to us and said, 'She wants you to receive it!' She was so excited to share it with all of us. It was the first time she had ever contributed to the meal."

Katie's life has also been touched. Katie still suffers the effects of a head trauma she sustained many years ago in an accident. Her family doesn't know how to handle her. The head injury affects her speech, and they don't have the patience to listen to her talk. This is very distressing to Katie, but Elizabeth is able to relate to her.

"Why am I here? Can God use me?" Katie asks.

"Katie, the Lord wants to use you despite your trials and challenges. Whatever disabilities you have, God wants to use you. I'm not just saying this, Katie. This is what happened to me, too. God wants to use you as much as He wants to use me. And He wants to use you in a powerful way. Isn't that wonderful?"

"Well, yeah. I don't really understand why, but it's still cool. I help Billie next door take out her trash because she has a walker and she can't take it out herself."

"Well, there you are. You see, God is using you to minister to your neighbors."

"And I take Cindy's trash out, too, because she doesn't feel good. So I take out her trash and Billie's trash and my trash. And I help Barbara when she needs things done around her house."

"You see, the Lord is showing you how He's using you!"

Katie and Elizabeth have now been meeting one-on-one for some time. Katie is ready to be baptized, and the whole house church will attend that celebration.

Scott is a huge part of what is going on. He and Elizabeth pray together before each of the neighborhood meals, asking that God will be glorified in what goes on. When people arrive, they all hold hands and bless the food before sharing in the meal together. Most of the ministry happens around the dining table. People share what is going on in their lives, and they talk about a passage from the Bible. They end their time together by praying for each other.

All the adversity has made Elizabeth into a strong and resolute woman of God. She loves to tell people about Jesus. Every time she goes out her front door, she considers it an opportunity to talk with others about Him.

Elizabeth still ends up in the hospital three or four times a year, mostly tied to complications from her transplant. Even though she's upset and sick and in pain, she knows God always has a divine appointment waiting for her.

"Lord, I don't want to go to the hospital! But Lord, may Your will be done. Use me there for your glory!"

The Holy Spirit always comes. Whoever she meets, whatever they are going through, she can identify with them and encourage them because of the challenges she has faced in her life. If they are ill, she shares with them and prays with them. If they have a loss, she ministers to their grief. No matter where she goes, there is some kind of ministry waiting for her.

This past Easter, Scott and Elizabeth planned to share Communion with their new church, but Elizabeth was in the hospital for more surgery. She was in a room with three others, one of whom, Adrienne, needed a liver transplant. The four patients in the room quickly became friends and the Lord orchestrated a deep sense of community.

On Easter morning, Scott brought in bread and wine to share with Elizabeth.

"We are going to share Communion together," they explained to the other patients. "Would you like to join us?"

It was not just the patients who joined with them. Along with their families and the nursing staff, 15 people in that room celebrated Easter together. Scott shared with them the meaning of the death and resurrection of Jesus. Adrienne listened intently.

There was something special about Elizabeth's relationship with Adrienne. She understood at a deep level what the young girl was going through. At the time of Elizabeth's discharge, Adrienne had to go into a small isolation room. She was devastated by this because she would lose the community they had shared.

Before they left the hospital, Scott and Elizabeth laid hands on Adrienne and prayed for her. The peace of God descended into the room in an almost tangible way. Adrienne prayed for them, too. They didn't realize this would be the last time they would see her. Adrienne died the following day.

"Your neighbor is not just the person in the next house. It can be the person in the hospital bed next to you, or the one beside you in the line in the grocery store," Elizabeth reflects. "That person could die tomorrow. What are we waiting for? The Great Commission means that we slow our lives down enough to see the ministry that is right in front of us. It's so simple, yet we make it so complicated."

Scott and Elizabeth continue to be amazed at how God works so simply and supernaturally as they care for the people around them. They persist in seeking God's will and counsel for the next step. Scott and Elizabeth know that obedience is the key to seeing the glory of God in their neighborhood, and they are determined to follow the Great Commission.

KEY THOUGHTS: "THE GREAT COMMISSION"

The Great Commission is the "Great Omission" in most of our churches today.

In the Great Commission (Matthew 28:18-20), Jesus commands His disciples "Go and make disciples of all nations, baptizing them in the name of the Father and of the Son and of the Holy Spirit, teaching them to obey all that I have commanded you. And lo, I am with you always, even to the end of the age."

The Great Commission is not an optional extra for Christians. Many of us live in Christian ghettos of our own making, without ever developing meaningful relationships with unbelievers. We believe the lie that friendship with people in the world will somehow contaminate us. So we avoid making relationships of any depth with those outside the church. But as it says in Romans 10, "How will they hear unless someone tells them?" (Verse 14) Admittedly, all of us are not evangelists, but all of us are to be witnesses to what He has done in our lives. (Acts 1:8) We have the life of Jesus within. If we ask the Lord for opportunity to share that life with others, He will delight to answer that prayer.

In the Great Commission, Jesus tells us to "*go.*" In most churches, even in our simpler expressions of church, we ask people to come: "Come to our special meeting; come to hear this incredible speaker!" So we ask people to cross a huge cultural divide and come into our religious meetings—where we get them to sit down and stand up to order, sing songs they do not know and then to give their lives to Christ. All of those things are totally foreign to them. Praise God, many people give their lives to Him in this fashion. However, Jesus instructed us to go to them. We are supposed to get out of our comfort zones, and make the effort to cross the barriers into their culture and touch then in a way that is relevant to them. Elizabeth, despite her immense physical obstacles, chooses to live this way.

The Great Commission tells us to make disciples of all nations. What is a nation? In all of our cities there are different segments of society that are basically untouched by church or the gospel (see Josh's story). We should be seeking the Lord on behalf of these people.

How do we make disciples of these groups? We are looking for far more than a "decision" or a "prayer of salvation." We are to make disciples, not mere converts. We are seeking a radical life change, a whole new way of living.

The Great Commission talks about making disciples of a nation. How will we know when a nation has been discipled? We are looking for the point when that people group or sub-culture is multiplying churches with indigenous (local) leaders without need of outside help.

Then we are to baptize the new believers. George Patterson was a missionary and church planter for many years and now mentors church planters. He has researched the subject of baptism and found that the dropout rate of new converts on the mission field is normally around 95%. However, this plummets to near zero if people are baptized quickly. (Obviously there may be reasons to delay baptism, such as sickness, or waiting for the river to thaw. The important thing is that baptism is not seen as something that has to be "earned.") In the New Testament, people were baptized on the same day that they repented and committed their lives to the Lord. For example, on the day of Pentecost, the three thousand new converts were baptized immediately. (Acts 2:41) There is no Scriptural precedent for delaying baptism until a person has been through the church's Christianity 101 program!

It is interesting that, in many nations where people are persecuted for becoming followers of Jesus, there are few, if any, repercussions if a person merely says that he has become a Christian. But when he is baptized, all hell breaks loose! It's as if Satan recognizes the strategic nature of baptism, even if we do not. Baptism is like a rite of passage between a person's old life and his new life in Christ. It is far more than just a step of obedience or an opportunity to witness to friends.

I recently led an interactive Bible study on the Great Commission at a conference. As we talked and studied, the Holy Spirit highlighted baptism. Many people cried tears of repentance as they realized they had not led people into immediate baptism following conversion.

Don't miss the strategic importance of baptism.

The Great Commission doesn't instruct us to learn all about Jesus' commandments, but to obey them. Big difference! If a new Christian learns early-on that he is to obey the will of God as soon as he understands it (whether it is from the written Word or from hearing the voice of the Lord in his heart), this gives him a foundation in his Christian walk that lasts the rest of his life.

In Romans 15:16, the writer says "I bring you (the Gentiles) the good news and offer you up as a fragrant sacrifice to God." We no longer go to the Temple to offer our sacrifices on the altar as they did in the Old Testament. But certain sacrifices are mentioned in the New Testament that we can offer to God now—for example, praise (Hebrews 13:15) or our own bodies (Romans 12:1). The offering of "the Gentiles" (unbelievers) is another. God is pleased when we "offer" Him the new disciples we have won to Christ.

Elizabeth is committed to living out the Great Commission where she lives. She seizes every opportunity she can with a daring, reckless faith to tell others the good news, and her life is bearing much fruit. If Elizabeth can do it, so can we!

JOSH'S STORY

Bearing much fruit

JOSH STORIES

John and Gloria's family love to tell "Josh stories." They laugh a lot. Sometimes they cry a little, and they remember...

They remember one Christmas Eve when Josh was seven years old. There were a lot of people in the house, but Gloria noticed Josh going to his room, weeping. She followed him.

"What's wrong, Josh?"

"I killed that turkey!" he kept saying. Gloria thought about the turkey meal they had just eaten.

"What turkey are you talking about?" But she couldn't make any sense out of what he was saying.

Later that evening when all their guests were gone, she went back to Josh.

"Josh, what happened?" she asked.

It turned out that their neighbors, who were out of town for the holidays, had a huge domestic turkey. The turkey escaped from its run and flew over the fence into their yard. Josh saw it and wanted to help. So he asked his father if he could use his snake catcher, planning to catch the turkey by the neck and lead it back to their yard.

The next morning, they discovered an enormous white turkey across the street, lying dead in their neighbor's front yard.

"Oh my gosh, John!" exclaimed Gloria. "He did kill a turkey. John, get that turkey out of here!"

They remember another instance, when Josh was five years old, getting a call from a friend.

"I was just at the Plaza shopping center and I saw Josh there, alone."

"What! You must be mistaken," replied Gloria. "Josh is in his room, playing."

But when they looked, he was not in the house and his little bicycle was missing. John rushed down to the shopping center a mile away; and sure enough, there he was!

"Josh, what are you doing?" they asked him.

"I want to buy a compass with that dollar Nana gave me," he replied.

"How did you get across the highway?"

"A man helped me cross the road."

"Josh, you let a stranger help you across the road?"

"Oh, he wasn't a stranger," Josh responded. "You always tell me, 'Don't get into a car with strangers,' and he wasn't in a car!"

Josh's parents remember another Thanksgiving they had a bunch of people in their home. It was cold, so they built a fire. But when they lit the fire, the house filled with smoke. They couldn't get the flue open. Finally, realizing there must be something in the chimney, they put the fire out. The next day, John and a friend climbed onto the roof and lowered a basket down the chimney. John knelt in the fireplace, reached into the flue and placed in the basket whatever he could feel in the chimney. When they raised the basket, they found coke bottles, cinder blocks, dead birds, all kinds of things Josh had dropped down the chimney. He knew the birds in the chimney shouldn't be there, so he thought he would be helping if he killed them. Josh had dropped a whole wheelbarrow full of stuff down there.

"I have a whole new respect for Josh," exclaimed John. "Anyone who could haul that much stuff onto the roof and drop it down the chimney has to have some strength. And he's only eight!"

Although Josh's antics as a young boy were "amusing," they soon took a dark turn. Eventually, it seemed Josh was constantly in trouble. He had his own agenda that seemed to always backfire on him. Once, he shot all the neighbor's windows out with his BB gun while trying to kill wasps from the nests under the eaves of the house. He thought he was taking care of a problem, and was quite unaware of the havoc he caused by breaking the windows.

John and Gloria were always careful not to leave him alone. If they did, someone would be there when they returned—either the police or the fire department. Josh called 911 one time just to see if the number worked! It did, and the fire truck came!

Josh marched to another drumbeat. A good-looking kid, he just didn't fit in; he was not like the other kids. He was always doing weird things. Right from the moment he was born, he was different, troubled. An irritable and unloving baby grew into a troubled child. Before he was born, the family was close. But as he grew older, he caused great division by pitting one family member against another. He saw through people and used their weaknesses to control them. He picked Gloria as the one he struck out against most. Counselors told them this was common with kids like Josh. He had an uncanny ability to know things about people. He knew if they were real or not. This is one of the problems he had with church; he sensed the hypocrisy. One of Gloria's friends commented, "He's like an old soul, he just knows things!"

Life at school was no different. Josh's disruptive behavior continually landed him in trouble with his teachers. Gloria remembers that every school year except Josh's 8th grade year, school officials called her almost every single day. In 8th grade, Josh respected a male teacher. He showed Josh tough love, and that year Josh made straight A's. But that was the only year he did well. John and Gloria took Josh to all kinds of counselors and psychiatrists, but none helped much.

The troubled child grew into a disturbed young man, and John and Gloria's life became a roller-coaster ride revolving around Josh.

AN INTRODUCTION TO GANG LIFE

By the time he was seventeen, Josh was in a special education program on the campus of an alternative school. That year, he told John and Gloria that he was a gang member. To start with, John and Gloria did not believe him. After all, he was a special education student. They were shocked to discover that he was riding the school bus with all the gang members who attended the alternative school, and was getting acquainted with them.

As time went on, Josh had more difficulty in school. Eventually

John and Gloria removed him from the public education system and started home schooling. Then kids from the neighborhood began coming to their house. Gloria was shaken when she realized that these kids, 12 years old and up, were not in school. They weren't skipping school; they had become "throwaway kids." The school system had somehow weeded them out, and they never went to school. They loved to hang out at John and Gloria's home because they knew they were welcome.

It was about this time that John and Gloria got involved in a home church. Every Sunday evening they loaded their van and made the hour-long journey to a church that met in the home of Tony and his wife. Once or twice, Josh came with them. He sensed that the people who were part of that little church lived what they said and were not playing games.

Josh never showed much interest in spiritual things. The most Gloria ever heard him say about his beliefs was, "I believe in God, and I also believe in the other guy. But I don't want anything to do with him (Satan)."

One Sunday afternoon, Gloria was in the kitchen fixing a dish to take to the church. Quite a few of the "throwaway kids" had been hanging around the house all weekend with Josh. Some of the girls came into the kitchen.

"What's that?" they asked Gloria, watching her spoon some cake mix into a pan.

"We are going to home church and this is for our potluck dinner," she replied.

"Can we go?"

"Sure, you can come with us."

"Well, what should we wear?" asked one of the girls.

"It doesn't matter what you wear. Wear what you have on!"

"Can we go right now?"

Then Gloria called Tony.

"Are you ready for this? We're taking gang members to church tonight!"

They crammed as many of the kids as they could, including Josh, into the van and drove to the meeting. All the kids seemed to enjoy the time, although Josh disrupted the meeting by walking up and down the stairs and making weird noises.

A few days later, Josh approached Gloria.

"Can we have one of those potlucks at our house?"

"Well I guess so," assuming he was talking about church.

Gloria called Tony.

"Would you be willing to meet with these kids up here?" she asked.

"Well, yes! If they want to, I'll come and be with them."

Two months later, both families could finally make it on a Sunday afternoon During the week leading up to the prearranged time, Gloria kept asking Josh, "Are your friends going to come or not?" But he was so dysfunctional that he couldn't pin down whether anyone would be there.

At 5:00 PM that Sunday afternoon, some of the kids showed up at the house. Gloria called Tony to let him know.

"Hold them off. Order in some pizza and I'll come right away," he said.

Tony sat on the patio with them and talked about the Bible. He told them they could ask him anything. The kids received what he said because he was non-judgmental. As he was leaving, they announced that they wanted to meet with him again some time.

EXCEPT A GRAIN OF WHEAT DIES...

Two days later Jimmy, a friend of Josh's oldest brother and an alcoholic, telephoned Gloria several times. He called from a hotel, and Gloria persuaded him to tell her his room number. Jimmy's brother had committed suicide a few years before in a hotel room, and Gloria didn't like the way Jimmy sounded. Later that afternoon when Gloria was picking up Josh and three of his friends, she passed the junky motel where Jimmy was staying.

"I'll just swing by here and check on Jimmy—he sounded really bad," she told Josh. She pulled in to the parking lot, and found his room. The door was not latched, so she pushed the door open and went in. Jimmy was sitting there with a noose around his neck.

Gloria rushed over to him.

"Jimmy!" she cried, pulling the noose over his head.

"My life is so useless!" he sobbed.

Gloria did not know what to say to him, so she just sat with her arm around his shoulders, not wanting to leave.

Soon, Josh came barging in, his blond hair tussled, mad because he had been left sitting in the car. He instantly perceived what was going on. As he walked across the room, Gloria looked at him and thought to herself, "Who is this?" She barely recognized him because his countenance was totally different. He walked over to Jimmy and put a hand on his shoulder.

"It's going to be OK, man," he said. Then turning to Gloria, he said, "Mom, go home and get Dad. I'll stay here with Jimmy." Gloria left.

"He spoke with such authority that I just did it," she later recalled. "I was so amazed because he never did anything responsible. I went home and got John and we both went back to the motel. When we arrived, Josh and Jimmy were standing in front, laughing and looking so good. I thought, 'I can't believe this. I can't believe Jimmy looks like this!'"

On the way back home in the car, Josh said to them, "Jimmy and I talked and Jimmy doesn't want me to end up like him. So I've made up my mind I'm going to quit smoking. I'm going to enroll in college, and tomorrow I'm going to mow the yard and show Dad I can be responsible."

Gloria was sitting in the back seat of the car, and she and John made eye contact in the rearview mirror when he said this.

"What's going on?" thought Gloria. "Josh is 17 years old and I've never heard him say anything like this before. He never does anything to please us. He's just not that kind of person. I can't believe I'm hearing him say these things! It's as if he's repenting for what he's done."

Late that evening, Josh and seven or eight of his friends were watching TV in his bedroom, a room John had created from their garage. Gloria was out having a cup of coffee with a friend. John had taken Jimmy home and then went to bed early. While John was sleeping, Josh crept into his parent's room and took his father's car keys. He unlocked the car and found a gun that was kept there.

Coming back into his bedroom, Josh carefully unloaded the gun, putting all the bullets in his pocket. (He had been taught how to handle guns.) He pointed the gun toward the TV screen, and pulled the trigger. There was a click.

"Quit doing that, Josh!" said one of the girls. "Your Dad's going to get up and find you with that gun and you'll be in big trouble!"

But Josh loved showing off. He kept playing with the gun, pointing it at one thing and then another and pulling the trigger.

"Quit it, Josh!" they said again.

Josh flopped down onto the couch. There was a sudden explosion, and Josh slumped backwards.

"Josh, now look what you've done!" The other kids thought he fired into the ceiling, and that he was acting like he was hit to scare them. In fact, when he fell backwards onto the couch, his elbow hit the arm of the couch, dislodging a bullet that was stuck in the barrel of the gun. With his finger on the trigger, the gun fired. The bullet went through Josh's forehead.

As soon as they realized what happened, the kids freaked out. They ran out of the garage to the front door and rang the doorbell, waking John.

"Josh shot himself," they cried.

It was too late. By the time Gloria came home, the road was filled with police cars and ambulances. John was standing alone in the front yard.

"Oh, no! What's Josh done now?" she thought. "I hope he hasn't hurt someone."

As Gloria stepped out of the car, John came up to her, tears running down his cheeks.

"Josh is gone!" he said.

Somehow Gloria was not surprised that his life had ended like this. His life wasn't like any other life. He had caused them so much grief, yet now his life was over.

In the middle of the night, Gloria called to let Tony and his wife know what had happened. The Lord clearly spoke through the Scriptures.

"Unless a grain of wheat falls into the ground and dies, it remains alone; but if it dies, it produces much grain." (John 12:24)

"Lord, bring Your glory out of this terrible situation," they prayed.

That night, John and Gloria talked together and decided they would not let this event ruin their marriage. They knew too many couples whose marriages had been destroyed by tragedy. They decided there would be no "what if" or "if only"—and above all, no blame. (Their relationship has actually grown closer since Josh's death.)

The memorial service for Josh was scheduled for a few days later, and John and Gloria asked Tony to speak.

"We'd like you to give an altar call," they told him. "The only thing that would make any sense out of Josh's death is if some of his friends find the Lord."

...IT BEARS MUCH FRUIT

A large group of Josh's friends from several different gangs came to the memorial service. John and Gloria found out later that Josh was a member of several gangs and always tried to be a peacemaker between them. As at least 50 gang members marched into the church building, one of the ladies of the church became very distraught.

"We can't have these kids here. They don't belong. Suppose they start fighting or breaking things up. They need to wait outside!"

"These kids are where they need to be. These are the kind of kids who need to be in church," one of the older men reassured her.

The gang members behaved well throughout the service. Tony told the group that Josh's last wish was that his friends would come to the "potluck Bible study" because he cared about their spiritual lives. The only thing that would make sense of his death was if they would give their lives to Jesus. Then he gave the altar call. Twenty eight kids responded! Each one signed a piece of paper so that John and Gloria could follow up with them. Jimmy was one of the kids who gave his life to Christ! Gloria still has that piece of paper. It is one of her most treasured possessions.

As the kids filed out of the church, each one presented Gloria with a rose.

"Oh, they're all so nice; they're bringing me flowers!" Gloria naively thought to herself. She did not realize at the time that if a gang member dies, it is a custom for the other members of the gang to each put a rose on the casket. Since this was a memorial service and there was no casket, they all gave their flowers to Gloria! Later she became much more familiar with how gangs work.

The gang kids requested they continue the potluck in memory of Josh. John and Gloria were willing to open their home. Word spread, and the following Sunday, more than 50 gang members crowded into John and Gloria's living room. John talked with some of the boys.

"OK, you leave your colors on the curb! There's to be no fighting here."

Week after week, the kids came. And week after week, more and more of them gave their hearts to Jesus. (John and Gloria estimate that around 100 of them eventually became Christians.) Many of their lives were transformed. There were frequent stories like this:

"I was really annoyed by someone this week, but instead of beating him up, I just walked away."

John and Gloria soon understood what a miracle this was. The gangs in that particular city were renowned for their aggression. Gang members were "beaten in" as their initiation into the gang, and "beaten out" if they left. Violence and crime was a way of life. Many of the guys were in jail or on probation, and many of the girls were pregnant or had young babies.

THE DEATH OF A GANG

The girlfriend of one of the gang leaders was one of the first girls to become a Christian. "Shaker" was in a lock-up situation in a Christian rehabilitation center. He accepted the Lord there. His girlfriend wrote to him and reported what was going on at the potlucks. And he replied with what the Lord was doing with him.

When "Shaker" was released, he also came to the Bible studies. At this point, the numbers thinned out some; since he was a gang leader, only his gang was able to come. At Christmas, the kids gave John and Gloria a Christmas ornament in the gang colors of pink and black—a sign of their acceptance.

At the beginning, Tony went to the potlucks every week. But it wasn't long before an ex-gang member, who had become a Christian a few years earlier, approached John and Gloria. Bobby had been a Satanist until Jesus radically transformed his life. He attended a large church in a nearby town. He had a heart for kids from his kind of background. So when he heard what was happening with the gangs, he asked if he could come and watch. The first time he came, he could hardly contain himself as he saw what the Holy Spirit was doing. He was so excited he wanted to take over right then. He began leading things when Tony wasn't there, and this evolved into him leading the group. Although he was young and not that mature, the kids responded well to him because he loved them.

John and Gloria took the kids on two retreats over the two years the group met together. The second one appeared to be a disaster. The retreat leaders spent much time in prayer and had their own pre-conceived ideas about what God would do. However, the kids rebelled and disobeyed, and the whole weekend was chaotic. But "Shaker" raked the kids over the coals when they came back home because of the way they had acted. He threw one of the kids out of the gang because of his disrespectful behavior at the retreat. He made the other troublemakers visit John and Gloria. One afternoon, all the kids who were involved came one by one; each one knelt at Gloria's feet and told her some of the specific things they appreciated about her and the way she cared for them.

"Thank you for the Easter baskets you prepared for us. We're sorry for the way we acted."

"Thank you for driving us down there."

They did the same to John.

"We felt so humbled," Gloria says of that time. "We were amazed at the integrity of the kids. We had expected and hoped for some kind of religious fervor from the weekend. It could have been just an emotional experience, but something far more lasting resulted. These kids live such harsh lives that they didn't respond to our taking them away the same way other kids would. "Shaker" showed them how they had erred and that they had to repent for the way they acted and learn to appreciate what we had done for them. It did not accomplish what we had hoped for, and yet the lesson they learned was far more valuable." She laughs. "I'll never forget those big tough gang members carrying around their Easter baskets!"

As the kids became Christians, one by one they stopped coming to the potlucks. They were leaving the gang, many of them without understanding why they didn't need it anymore. Because this was a gang Bible study, and they were no longer gang members, they just didn't show up. Even the gang leaders didn't know what happened to them. Some of them became involved in local churches.

The potlucks ended because the gang disbanded. No kids were left in the gang—they had all become Christians! Josh was a seed that literally fell to the ground and died, and a great harvest resulted.

KEY THOUGHTS: BEARING MUCH FRUIT

In preparation for this chapter, I asked Gloria, "How much of Josh's story would you like told? Would you like me just to say, 'He was a troubled young man'?"

"Oh no!" she replied. "You can tell the whole story. I would like to encourage those who deal with a kid like Josh to know that God can use people like that.

"Why did God allow us to have a child like that? We spent every moment trying to help him, and then he was gone. Someone once asked us, 'Is your life the same as before you had Josh?' We learned so much through dealing with him. God uses all kinds of things to teach us and to grow us into what He wants us to be. Life is a tapestry, and Josh was a part of ours. I don't know if Josh could have ever functioned as a normal adult. Maybe that's why the Lord allowed this.

"Some of the kids still stay in touch, and many of their lives remain changed. One of them has even gone into the ministry!

"We found out after Josh died that he did a lot of loving things for people that we never knew about. And then look at what God did through his death! All these kids' lives changed because of Josh. God brought such incredible glory through his death. I want his story to live on and to continue to bear fruit—that's the greatest memorial he could have."

It is difficult for people like Josh and his friends to get involved in our legacy churches. They find them boring and irrelevant. In many of those churches, they are not welcome. Their language may be offensive, their behavior disturbing. They do not fit into our nice middle-class church culture.

The Great Commission tells us that we are to make disciples of all nations. What is a nation? The Greek words used are "ta ethne" from which we get our word "ethnic." So the idea is more of a people grouping or subculture than of a nation in the conventional sense of the word. These are distinct segments of society, each with their own culture, language and customs. In our city, for example, there are many different sub-cultures. They include students, skaters, yuppies, the elderly, mall rats (young teenagers who hang out in shopping malls), club kids (teenagers and young twenty-somethings who spend their nights around the clubs and bars), as well as the poor, and all the different nationalities, to name just a few. Some ethnic groups, subcultures and interest groups have easy access to the gospel while others, like Josh and his gang friends, are quite isolated from it. Although our city may appear to have many churches, really the only segment of society that is adequately churched is white, middle-class families. Sadly, the majority of the other groups mentioned above no longer darken the doors of our churches.

However, many in these groups are desperate for some reality and meaning in their lives. Given the opportunity, they will respond to our genuine overtures of friendship. But they see straight through us if our only motivation for approaching them is to preach the gospel. How can we be content to remain in our pews—or on our couches? Let's ask the Lord to open our eyes to the opportunities around us. Let's take some action!

ROSA –
A PERSON OF
PEACE

Luke 10 principles

PRAYER WALKING

I (Felicity) was gazing out of my bedroom window at the big oak trees, and watching a couple of squirrels chasing each other along the branches when I heard the words:

"You are to prayer-walk Oltorf."

"Where did that come from?" I wondered. The words seemed to come out of nowhere during one of my regular morning times with the Lord. But experience has taught me over the years that a thought like that from "right field" is one of the ways Jesus most commonly speaks to me.

I would like to tell you that I obeyed instantly, but it was probably a couple of months before I finally got around to walking Oltorf, a street about twenty minutes from our home. On my second day of walking, I came across a low-income housing project called Springfield. A large sign at the entrance stated that loitering was forbidden and anyone on the property must carry an ID. As I wandered between the run-down row houses, past the dumpsters and the abandoned cars, praying for the people who lived there, the Lord spoke again.

"You are to start a church here!"

On the way back to the car, I met one of the neighbors of the complex, and we started chatting.

"Do you see that hole?" he asked, pointing to a small hole in the fence. "That's a bullet hole from a drive-by shooting. And that car," he continued, waving his arm in the direction of a flashy sedan that was driving past, "belongs to one of the drug dealers on Springfield."

Back in our home church that weekend, I shared what I sensed the

Lord to be saying, and a group formed with the express commitment of praying for the people who lived on Springfield. Occasionally we got together to pray, and once or twice we actually prayer-walked through the housing complex. But mostly we prayed on our own.

About six months later, Tony and I were driving along Oltorf.

"Why don't we prayer-walk Springfield? We have some spare time this morning."

We parked some distance away and made our way into the housing complex. What I did not realize was that Tony specifically prayed that we would meet our "person of peace" that day.

All of a sudden, the skies darkened and there was a torrential downpour. We couldn't make it back to the car, so we dashed for shelter under a balcony where two middle-aged, Hispanic women sat in lawn chairs, chatting. As our conversation with them moved on from the weather, one of them asked why we were there. I guess we didn't fit the local profile.

"We're here to pray for your neighborhood," we told them.

It turned out that Rosa and her sister were born into a Catholic family, and would die Catholic. Yet they never planned to darken the door of a Catholic church again because of an incident many years ago. However, they knew God was real. Rosa told a remarkable story about one of her children becoming seriously ill when he was very young and experiencing an angelic encounter and a dramatic healing.

As the rain slowed to a drizzle, Tony asked,

"Would it be OK if we came by from time to time to pray about some of the needs in your family?"

It was that simple. A couple of times a week we went to Rosa's house and prayed for the needs in her family and in the housing complex. We didn't stay long, just 15 to 20 minutes. And God began to answer prayer. Rosa had been trying to get welfare checks for two years, and a couple of weeks after we prayed, the checks began coming. We developed a real friendship with Rosa, and learned more about her family and some of the pressures they faced as they lived in the projects.

About six weeks later, we asked Rosa if she would like to bring together some of her family so that we could tell them about Jesus, too.

It was at this point we made a big mistake.

That very week, Rosa introduced us to a lady who lived a few doors down from her.

"You'll like Angela," she told us. "She's like you."

Sure enough, Rosa introduced us to a radical, radiant, on-fire Christian. Angela was soundly converted from many years of drug addiction, and that very week had gone from HIV positive to HIV negative following prayer from her church. What's more, her house reflected the fact that she had been a Christian for a few years; everything was orderly, and quiet worship music played in the background.

"This would be a great environment for Rosa's family," we thought.

So we gathered with Rosa for the first time in Angela's apartment, and it couldn't have been a bigger disaster! You see, Angela's church believed in using only the King James Version of the Bible. We had given Rosa a very simple version, and everything during the study was interpreted to and from King James English.

When we got back home, we were discouraged. Our time together didn't go well, and none of Rosa's family came.

"Where did we go wrong, Lord?" we asked.

Then we remembered Luke 10, where it specifically tells us to stay in the home of the person of peace and not move from house to house.

"Lord, we're so sorry," we prayed. "Please get us out of this one!"

LIVES TRANSFORMED

That very week, Angela was given a home outside of the projects. (She had been praying for this for months.) The next week, we returned to Rosa's house, which was chaotic but filled with love. Rosa has a heart the size of Texas—no one is a stranger in her home because of her amazing capacity to love people.

And her family started coming. Rosa was the first one to give her heart to the Lord. She did this quite simply, as we shared with her in her living room. Her life was so transformed that other family members saw the difference. Two of her sisters followed, then a couple of her kids, various nephews, nieces, grandkids and other family members. Other families from Springfield also attended. At one point, 35 people were crammed into her tiny apartment, sitting on the floor, up the stairs and in the kitchen. Eventually two other groups started from that one in other projects (although for various reasons, they did not continue long term).

Back in England, we worked in that kind of environment for many years. We watched the Lord perform miracles time and time again with people who had family members in prison, others on drugs or with drinking problems and families where all the kids had different fathers. Springfield was no different. Lives were transformed before our eyes. James, Rosa's youngest son, a talented rapper and 18 years old at the time, is a case in point.

Shortly after we started meeting at Rosa's, James told us why he could never become a Christian. A group of friends had been there for him since he was a kid; he knew that if he was put in a situation where he had to choose between his friends and Jesus, he would have to choose his friends. Norman, a friend of ours from England with a gift of insight from the Holy Spirit, visited the next week and had a word for James.

"James, Jesus loves the way you are such a good friend," Norman told him.

After donating blood the following week, James was told that he needed to make an appointment with the doctor because tests revealed some abnormalities in his blood. Of course, James feared the worst. So he told the Lord,

"If You will spare my life, You are going to be the One who has my honor and my respect from this day on!"

It turned out to be a very minor problem, but James kept his word to the Lord. "Lord, from this day on, You are the one who has all my honor and my respect." Not only that, but over the next few days, he contacted all his friends and told them, "From this day on, my honor and respect belong to Jesus. If I ever have to choose between you and Jesus, I will choose Him!"

Our times together at Springfield were always interesting! Let me describe one of my favorite gatherings.

We always started our times together with a meal, an event that at times takes on the elements of a stampede. On this particular occasion, we had barely finished the meal when a fight broke out between two of the kids. (They take that verse about resisting to the point of shedding blood very literally!) James took the trouble-maker upstairs and was dealing with him. He believed that if this kid behaved badly around the wrong person, he could get shot in that environment. Rosa got involved, and then James and Rosa disagreed on how to handle the kid. (This is church!) The kids finally were outside and the adults were sitting in the living room when James asked a question.

"How do you handle it when you hate someone?"

A 40-minute discussion followed about how a Christian handles hatred, how to discipline kids, and what to do when Christians disagree. We shared Bible passages and experiences together, and prayed for each other. Then the kids came in, and we had a time of praise together. They love to sing and worship. At one point I looked up, and two kids about nine and eleven years old, were singing their hearts out with their eyes closed. It may not have been the most in-tune worship, and it was certainly loud. But I thought to myself, "Jesus, You're here, and You love this!"

We experienced many miracles at Rosa's house. That was part of the problem, and the reason for another major mistake we made. Things were so exciting, we didn't want to leave. We knew it was important that the group be led by people from the projects. Eventually, when all the outsiders pulled out, Rosa was devastated.

"I feel like you don't love me any more," she confessed.

It took quite a while for the group to recover. But now, three years after its original start, James is leading the church in Rosa's house. We keep in close touch with both him and Rosa, and God continues to work!

KEY THOUGHTS: LUKE 10 PRINCIPLES

All over the world, the Lord is using the passage from Luke 10:1-9 as a pattern for making disciples and starting churches. Major church planting movements are happening in both India and China today with thousands of churches being planted each week; Luke 10 principles play a key part in all of them. But God isn't just working overseas. The story of Rosa and Springfield directly parallels Luke 10. So let's take a closer look at the passage.

- Verse 1: Jesus sent out 70 disciples, two by two, to all the towns and villages where He planned to go. Jesus obviously had a master plan for reaching the region and he sent the disciples to specific towns. They were to go two by two (not singly and not in larger teams) and the exciting thing was that Jesus was going to follow close behind. Notice the parallels with the way the Lord led us to Springfield.
- Verse 2: Jesus told them that the harvest is great but the laborers are few. Jesus told the disciples to pray to the Lord of the harvest that He would send out laborers into the harvest.

According to Jesus, the problem is not the harvest, but the laborers. In other places He tells us that the harvest is ready now. How often do you hear people complain about the hardness of their area? But according to Jesus, that is not the problem. It is the shortage of laborers that prevents the harvest from being gathered in. And He had 35 teams going out—41 if you also count the 12 disciples. Most churches would be overjoyed if they had that many apostolic church planters! Yet Jesus calls this number "few." What would He consider "enough" or "many?" Perhaps hundreds of teams for one area are what He desires.

Prayer is the key to seeing God act. If we want to see God move by multiplying simple or organic churches, we are deceiving ourselves if we think it will come cheap! We need to pray the price.

Alex Vander Griend tells about a church in Phoenix that conducted an interesting experiment a few years ago. Someone in the church picked 160 names out of the phone book and divided the names into two groups. The intercessors in the church prayed for all the names in one group, but did not pray for the other group. After 90 days of prayer, church members called all 160 homes, asking for permission to come and pray for any needs in the families. Of the 80 that were not prayed for, only one person invited church members to come. Of the 80 that were prayed for, 69 invited someone to come over; of those, 45 asked them into their homes to pray. We should never underestimate the power of prayer. (*The Praying Church Idea Book* by Douglas A. Kamstra)

Another thing is interesting about this verse. The disciples prayed for workers in the places they were going to visit. We will see later in the passage that they were praying for the "people of peace." So the laborers God would use to bring in a harvest in each village were people from that village –i.e., the resources for the harvest are in the harvest. This is a huge paradigm shift for the average Christian.

In Springfield, that meant God wanted to use people who were not yet Christians to change Springfield. Rosa and James have proven to be the workers for that harvest field.

- Verse 3: Jesus tells the disciples to go. The New Testament church was a "going" church. Instead, we ask people to come to our churches.
- Verse 4: The disciples are told not to take anything with them. The material resources are in the harvest too. But this is not the only reason. The disciples didn't plan to stay long term.

The story of Springfield provides another lesson here. We caused major problems when we did not quickly hand over leadership to someone from the complex. We bred an unhealthy dependence on the outsider, which nearly shipwrecked the whole church. (Praise God, He covers our mistakes!) In rapidly multiplying church-planting movements, leadership is handed over quickly—within a matter of days to weeks—while the new leader is closely mentored by the outsiders.

• Verses 5 and 6: We are looking for a person who will invite us into their home. This is likely to be our "person of peace." A person of peace is someone who has a circle of influence, and they will give us access to those people. Rosa was our person of peace on Springfield. She gave us an entrance to her family, and she knew everyone in her complex. The person of peace is often a person of reputation, whether good or bad. Lydia, from Acts 16, was a person of peace. But so was the woman at the well, whose reputation was not so savory (John 4).

- Verse 7: We should stay in that house, eating and drinking what is set before us. What is the reason for sharing food? We are creating relationships. Not only that, but when we eat with someone in their home, we enter into their culture; we aren't asking them to join our culture. This may not be a comfortable process. For obvious reasons, we are much more at ease in our own environment. This verse also tells us that we should not go from house to house. (What does that say about door-to-door evangelism?)

- Verse 8: Eating again! Something about this is extremely important. Note that so far, we have not preached or engaged in any other form of direct evangelism. All we have done is identify the person of peace and eat with them.

- Verse 9: We are to heal the sick. We need to expect the Lord to intervene in their lives in a supernatural way. Only then do we have the right to speak to them about the Kingdom of God. Because they have watched the Lord work, they will be open. Seeing Rosa's welfare checks come within two weeks of praying for her unlocked the door for us at Springfield.

Many of the stories in this book demonstrate how answered prayer is a key and one of the primary ways to start a new church. If we ask God for opportunities to pray for people's needs, He will give them to us. Of course, there is a challenge to our faith in praying. We love the way John Wimber used to spell faith: R-I-S-K. It is risky business to step out in faith and offer to pray for someone. But God delights in answering that kind of prayer.

The people in the amazing stories that we heard in India (such as the middle-aged housewife starting 50 churches in one year) use this Luke 10 passage as their pattern.

The housewife waits on the Lord to tell her which village to enter. She prayer-walks that village until someone invites her into their home. Assuming this is the person of peace, she eats and drinks and creates a friendship with them. Then she asks if they know anyone who needs prayer. When the Lord shows up with healing or deliverance, she takes that opportunity to tell them about the Kingdom of God, and some become believers. She then moves on to the next village, while other Christians follow up with the new disciples.

FRANK'S STORY

The Holy Spirit leads us

DIRECTION FROM GOD

Frank and his wife just celebrated their 51st wedding anniversary, but things haven't always gone smoothly for them. During a rough patch late in their marriage, Frank and his wife separated for a few years. During that period, Frank sensed the Lord leading him to move to a city in the Midwest. He always wanted to live in the inner city, and this was his opportunity. So Frank bought an old house for zero down, and covered part of the house payments by renting rooms in the house.

For some years before moving to the Midwest, Frank was the consulting chaplain at a drug and alcohol rehab center in Southern California. While there, he became convinced that huge numbers of potential church leaders are in jail, homeless or addicted—not to be found in any organized Christian movement. So he brought men from the rehab center he felt were called by God for ministry to live with him and be trained. When he and his wife reunited, he kept the extra house for these men to live in, even though he spent most of his time back on the West coast.

Three years ago, when Frank was preparing to move back to that same Midwestern city, he pictured a face in his mind while he was praying.

"Who can that be?" he thought to himself. "It's nobody I recognize."

The face Frank pictured was distinctive. With dark hair drawn back from his face and a mustache, the man looked Italian to Frank.

A few days later, while driving the long miles to scout out the city, Frank "heard" a voice speaking to him.

"Go to the corner of Crockett and Carthage."

Somehow, Frank knew he would meet the person he had "seen" in a restaurant near that intersection.

Upon his arrival in town, Frank drove to that location. It was in a bad part of town. The houses were run-down, and abandoned cars littered the street.

"There must be a restaurant here somewhere," he said to the friend traveling with him.

Nothing even resembled a restaurant. Then Frank noticed a dark building with a dim light over the door. A faded sign on the door read, "Bar Open." It was a cheerless-looking place, not a good start to his venture.

"There's no way I'm going into that dive," his friend announced.

Frank parked the car, got out and locked it carefully. Picking his way through the trash on the sidewalk, he made his way to the door and opened it. It was almost black inside, and the atmosphere reeked of decay, smoke and stale beer. There was a bar in front of him. A couple of men sitting on bar stools gazed vacantly into the distance. As he entered, everyone turned to look at him; they obviously were not used to strangers. (Was this a cop?) Behind the bar in a sort of lounge area, the ceiling was coming down. A lady was clearing the dirty glasses and emptying cigarette butts from the ash trays. Frank made his way back to her.

"Is there a restaurant near here?" he asked the lady, who was wiping a table with a dirty cloth. She turned out to be the owner of the place.

"I'm just about finished here," she said. "There's a café a couple of blocks away. If you follow me in your car, I'll take you there."

As she finished her work, she asked Frank some questions about what he was doing. Frank shared with her that God was leading them to live in that city. He talked to her a bit about church.

Frank followed the lady as she drove past a run-down looking storefront a couple of blocks away. It had a sign, "Bistro and Eatery," hanging in the window. It was obviously the place she meant. It was getting late by this time. So rather than go into the café then, Frank left and found a bed for the night.

The next morning, Frank drove back to the restaurant. It was not much better in daylight. He pushed open the dirty, glass door to the café.

There, through an archway, he saw a person sitting.

"It's him!" Frank exclaimed to himself. "It's the man in my picture!"

Frank walked between the tables, covered with red-checked plastic cloths, and made his way toward the man. But as he rounded the corner beside the archway, he did a sudden double-take. The "man" was wearing a dress!

In fact, it was not a man. Nora turned out to be a lady, slightly balding with her hair combed straight back, and the mustache was real. Frank was overwhelmed.

Walking up to her, Frank said, "When I was praying the other day, I saw you. Can I talk to you for a while?"

He sat down opposite her at the table. As they talked together, Frank learned more about Nora's life. Nora was what many would consider a throw-away sort of person, badly damaged in many ways. Her husband was a full-blown alcoholic who washed dishes in the restaurant. Nora herself was only in her fifties, although she looked much older. Throughout her life, she had been appallingly rejected. You see, Nora is half Native American and half black. She was rejected by Native Americans because she is half black, and treated the same way by African Americans.

Frank and Nora also talked about Nora's religious beliefs. She had been ostracized in the churches she tried to attend. Although she wanted to believe in God, she didn't believe He heard her prayers.

"How about I come to your house to talk with you and your husband about how Jesus can be more involved in your lives," Frank suggested. That day, Frank visited her house and met some of her beautiful grandchildren. That evening, they held a "meeting" for Nora, her husband and the grandchildren before her daughter came to pick up the kids.

Frank has met with Nora several times, and knows that the Lord is moving in her life. But even more importantly, Frank has learned that following the promptings of the Holy Spirit are a key to this life of adventure.

NON-RELIGIOUS CHURCH

Remember the house that Frank bought two years earlier? Three or four men were still living there who wanted to follow Jesus. All of the men came out of various addictions and problems, but were learning to live and serve together. That house has become the center of a new church, and is a marvelous backdrop for what God is doing.

The first meetings centered on a neighbor's birthday. People from the neighborhood wouldn't come to a normal simple church meeting, but everyone loved birthdays. It was a great excuse to draw them together. After a meal and birthday cake, they prayed for and blessed the person with the birthday. Often, the Lord gave a prophetic word for them and wonderful things happened. Following this kind of experience, they were much more willing to get involved.

Andy, a young man who used to be a resident in the California rehab center, is another big factor in what is happening there. Following the surrender of his life to Jesus, Andy went to a Bible school and then joined Frank. Since Frank lives with his wife on the West coast, Andy has become the main leader of the house church.

Andy really identifies with the young people in the neighborhood. He plays baseball with the kids and goes to the park with them. He even owns a pit bull—the dog of choice in their neighborhood—that helps him reach out to others. This has been very successful, and he has gained acceptance with a number of other dog owners. Several of the youth have become Christians. A couple of teenagers were baptized in a swimming pool. Others have been baptized in a kids' wading pool in the basement of the house.

It is wonderful what is happening there. Seven or eight people regularly get together on a Sunday, all of whom were non-Christians before. Some of them are growing like wildfire. A couple in their sixties, whom Frank never expected to embrace Jesus, has found the Lord. The wife, who had been illiterate all her life, is learning to read so she can study her Bible.

Their times together are full of life, and tend to be non-religious and unstructured. They share a meal together each week, and talk about things going on in their lives. They pray for one another and care for one another. Nobody puts on a phony front. People are real with each other and appreciate what God is doing with them.

Frank's vision for training leaders from tough backgrounds is coming to pass. The new church is proving to be a great training ground for them.

God loves to lead His people, and He has led Frank to a ripe harvest field.

GHTS: THE HOLY SPIRIT LEADS US

ı likes to say that programs are what the church
ın the Holy Spirit leaves!

le to say He did only what He saw the Father
do and spoke only what He learned from the Father. (John 5:19,
20; John 8:28) The same can be true for us. We need to learn
to recognize God's activities and how to hear His voice.

How do we know what God is doing? Someone mentions a
problem to you. You ask them, "Have you ever thought of praying about this situation?" They reply, "I feel like my prayers
are just hitting the ceiling." Here is an open door to a spiritual
conversation. This is God at work!

In Luke 10:1-9, the passage on which we base much of what
we do, Jesus sends the 70 disciples to all the towns and villages
He plans to visit (see verse 1). Jesus told the disciples where they
were supposed to be going. We need to hear from Jesus where
He wants us to make disciples and where He plans to build His
church. With which sub-culture should we be working? On
which apartment complex should we focus our prayer?

This implies an ability to hear the voice of God. This is a
skill that can be learned. For example, I could be in a room of
50 people who are all talking, but I could instantly distinguish
the voice of my husband, Tony. The reason? I have spent much
time with him and recognize his voice. In John 10:4, Jesus says
"The sheep follow him (the shepherd) because they know his
voice." The way to learn to hear Jesus' voice is to spend time
with Him.

Many years ago I did a considerable amount of counseling.
I tried to wait on the Lord for a while before I met with the
person needing help. I prayed for them (often in tongues), and
then I wrote what I sensed the Lord saying to me about their
situation. After I had spent time with them, I went back to
see if what I thought the Lord said to me was relevant to their
situation. Usually, 85 to 90 percent of the time, it was. Over

the years, I have learned to hear His voice. For me, the voice of Jesus often comes through a thought (or a picture in my mind) that seems to come out of nowhere!

Hearing the Lord's voice also helped cut considerably the time involved in counseling. For example, I remember a young girl once asked me after a meeting to help her because she was depressed. As we walked to a secluded corner, I quietly asked the Lord what the problem was. He gave me the impression that she had been sexually abused by her father when she was a child. It took two questions to arrive at the root of her problem. "Tell me about your relationship with your father," and "Did he abuse you in any way?" (Note that I did not say, "The Lord told me you were sexually abused by your father." It is embarrassing if you get it wrong, and it also gives the person an easy way out if they don't want to admit the truth of what you are saying.)

As individuals, and as churches, we can learn to recognize His voice. Just imagine church run on these principles! As an individual hears God speak, they obey His voice, and the Holy Spirit becomes the one to orchestrate the activity. As a church discovers the mind of Christ, (I Corinthians 2:16), they follow Him, and the Body of Christ grows.

Let's learn to hear His voice, and then obey Him as He leads us.

Another principle comes out of Frank's story. For many people, the church is the biggest stumbling block to following Jesus. But in the book of Acts, we see the opposite. There was something very winsome about the believers in the New Testament church. (Acts 2:47; Acts 5:13, 14)

It is obvious that what happens in Frank's world is noticeably non-religious. For far too many Christians, life is a rulebook of "do's and don'ts" – especially the "don'ts!" Jesus didn't die to give us a set of rules! He died that we might have life—abundantly. (John 10:10) When we become Christians, God gives us a new nature, a heart of flesh with His laws already written on it. (Hebrews 8:10) For us now, if we are walking close to

Jesus, what comes naturally is pleasing to God. Religion stifles life; legalism is deadly!

If we give unbelievers the impression that life is restrictive because we are Christians, that God is sitting up in heaven with a big stick waiting to pounce on us if we color outside the lines, this is hardly good news! Why would they want to join us? But if they are attracted to the life within us, if they see that we experience a joy and a peace even when things are going wrong, they will want to know more. That kind of Christianity is contagious; it can transform communities.

SAM'S STORY

"Good soil"

"I'M TOO BAD FOR GOD TO LOVE ME"

"I want to turn myself in. I've committed a crime that you need to know about. Is there a detective I can talk to?"

Sam's life is an open book. He willingly shares his story with anyone, because it brings such glory to Jesus.

Life was tough growing up for Sam. At the age of four, Sam contracted scarlet fever. His mother was pregnant at the time, and couldn't be in the same room because of the risk of infection. His father took care of her and also couldn't go near him. Sam slept on a sofa in the living room—that's where he lived alone and where he almost died. An aunt came to look after him a couple of hours each day. His older sister put food on a tray with wheels and pushed it into the room so he could eat. Other than that, he had no real human contact for several weeks.

"It's unlikely he's going to make it through the night," he overheard the doctor telling his aunt one day.

"I must have done something real bad for God to let this happen to me," was his conclusion.

After he recovered, the family moved to California, and Sam never saw his aunt again. He acted out in ways that must have been very frustrating for his parents, and that is when his father started beating him. His father was very physically abusive and sometimes beat Sam with a belt so badly that he couldn't go to school for weeks. His father believed in harsh discipline. But after every beating, he told Sam, "I'm only doing this because I love you." The effect on Sam was devastating.

Sam used to go behind his house where the sewer opened under the street. He squeezed his slim frame through a small manhole, climbed down into the sewers and crawled as far back in the pipes as he could.

"God, please will you stop my Dad from loving me!" he would beg.

At the age of 12, Sam went to his first Holy Communion in the Catholic Church. The nuns at the church taught him that if he took the bread and wine in an unworthy manner, he could get sick or die. Sam was scared because he was sure that he was unworthy. But the fear of humiliating his Dad was even greater. He knew that if he didn't take communion, he would get a beating. He went to the altar, but as the priest was about to put the bread onto his tongue, Sam fainted. As he walked out of the church after coming to, his sister looked at him and said, "I thought God struck you dead because you're so bad!" This reinforced Sam's sense that God was rejecting him.

When his parents divorced a few years later, Sam had fits of anger and would explode on his sisters without cause. One day, his older sister threw herself across his younger sister to protect her from his rage; he saw then what he had become.

"I will never, ever touch another person in anger," he vowed, deeply hurt as he realized what he had done. He has kept that vow to this day.

Sam's mom soon remarried. His new stepfather was a very hard man. He didn't hit Sam, but he yelled at him constantly. At the age of 16, his mother asked him to leave home. So he went to live with his Dad.

When he was just under 17, Sam joined the Navy. He used to hitchhike from where he was stationed in San Diego to L.A. One day, a man picked him up who was a friend of a friend. It turned out to be a set-up, and the man drugged and raped Sam. When he returned to the base that same day, Sam found a letter from his mom saying she disowned him as her son.

Something in Sam died that day.

LEGALISM KILLS

At the age of 18, Sam married a beautiful Mexican girl from Texas. By this time, he was extremely rebellious, and was drinking and using orange sunshine (LSD), speed and marijuana mixed with elephant tranquilizers. A year and a half later, he was discharged from the Navy.

One night, his wife's brothers and cousins turned on him. They wanted to start a gang, and Sam was considered an outsider because he wasn't Mexican. When he told them he didn't want to join the gang, they started yelling at him. His brother-in-law, who held a grudge against him for not being Mexican, threw a chair and hit his left eye. It swelled immediately.

Sam's wife ran for the car and she and Sam sped off. Although Sam and his wife were unaware of it, his wife's family members followed them. They blocked Sam's car in the driveway of his own home with their car. They pulled him from the car, and three of them held him down while another went to look for a pipe to beat him. His head was pinned to the ground in a way that forced him to look at a church bus.

"You've run life your way up until now. Why not try doing it My way?" God seemed to say to him.

Somehow with that thought, he had the strength to get away. When the police arrived, he did not press any charges because his wife was crying and begged him not to.

But in that brief moment, God had come into Sam's life. From that point on, he knew Jesus as his Savior. However, he assumed that living a holy life was up to him. For the next six years, Sam's Christianity was a severe and unrelenting rulebook of dos and don'ts to obey. He couldn't do it. For the last year and a half of that time, Sam's church heavily controlled every detail of the members' lives by what was called "shepherding." His whole family was very committed to that church and was always available to do whatever was needed. But as time went on, he could see this was damaging his family. So he trained others to take over his church responsibilities, and finally went to see his pastor.

"My wife and I are considering leaving the church," he told him.

"We feel that God is leading us elsewhere and we need to find another church." The pastor looked at him unsympathetically.

"You will never amount to anything in life because you're leaving my umbrella of protection," he pronounced.

Sam was determined to prove the pastor wrong. He resolved that his life would amount to something; so he moved into the business world, determined to succeed. He became involved politically, and developed a number of programs in hospital circles. He became very well known and respected among his peers and superiors. He climbed to the position of facility director of a hospital. His office walls were covered with training certificates and licenses. Sam made good money, and people were impressed. However, his family life was going downhill fast.

Sam received a phone call late one night while he was sleeping.

"Sam, you'd better get down to the hospital. Your son, Ben, has been shot. He's in critical condition and we're not sure he's going to make it."

As family life deteriorated, their oldest son Ben had become involved in gang life. A member from a rival gang shot him, and now his life was in serious danger. He actually died twice in the ambulance on the way to the hospital and once in the emergency room. But each time, God brought him back. The final time, Ben told them later, he looked up and saw a huge doctor standing over him. He felt a hand on his chest, and the doctor looked up and prayed, "Lord, please save this stupid little punk!" That prayer saved his life. (The doctor later became a good friend.)

The bullet ripped through Ben's esophagus, and the extent of the damage was not known for four days. By that time his heart and aorta had become affected. He needed another major surgery to repair the damage, and was in the hospital for three weeks. Miraculously, Ben fully recovered.

But the gang members who shot Ben wouldn't leave his family alone. Sam tried to work as normal. But he had an overwhelming fear all the time that the gang was out to get the whole family and would be coming to do a drive-by shooting.

So Sam sent the family out of state to stay with one of his wife's cousins, while he remained behind for two months to close out his job. He sent money to the family. But when he joined them, he found that all the money had been given to his wife's cousin. Then Ben and his wife's cousin got into a fight. The cousin threw them out, and they were on the streets with no place to stay. This happened to coincide with the worst snow storm the area had seen in decades.

The family ended up in a Salvation Army Family Safe Center. They lived there for two months until Sam was able to find a job and start over again. This time he worked as the manager of a crew that set up modular office spaces. He climbed the corporate ladder again, but inside his heart was dead. As things in his family continued to deteriorate, Sam assumed—just as he did when he was four years old with scarlet fever, or during his first Communion—that God was angry with him.

Sam started doing things he thought might take away the emptiness inside, but his focus was totally on himself. He met a 12–year-old girl and had a sexual encounter with her. He was 38.

FROM DEATH TO LIFE

The reality of what he had done jolted Sam to his senses. He finally saw himself for who he was. He left his family. He felt so bad about what he did that he wanted to take his life, and twice attempted to do so.

The first attempt was through a car wreck...that failed. On the second try, he went to a river, planning to jump off a cliff onto the rocks below. The current slammed his body to the bottom of the river, pulled him back to the surface again and he missed the rocks. He was so hurt and angry with God that he cursed Him.

"Why won't you let me die?"

Sam was still wet when he arrived at The Union Gospel Mission. After he had been there for a couple of days, the man running the dayroom asked him into his office.

"What brings you to the Mission, Sam?" he asked him.

On the spur of the moment, Sam decided to tell him everything he had done.

"I wanted him to hate me so much. It would have given me strength to go out and finish taking my life," he later admitted. But after hearing Sam's confession, the man said:

"Sam, a month ago I would have called you scum. But today I know God's love differently, and I welcome you as my brother!" He walked over to him and gave him a hug.

Sam's life changed completely that day. It was the best experience he had ever known. For the first time in his life, he experienced real love—unconditionally. He met other people at the Mission who gave him a similar welcome. This gave him the strength to call out to God. One day he went into the Mission chapel alone.

"God, if you will clean up my life inside and outside, I will go anywhere and do anything. But You have to do the work. I've already proven I can't."

When Sam got up from his knees, he felt clean—like he was able to start life again with a fresh slate. But deep in his spirit he knew God wanted him to turn himself in. He called the detectives, and they asked him to come to the station to take a recording of his confession. They didn't know about any crime, so they just let him talk.

"Wow, Sam!" said the detective. "We won't try to pretend we know what you're going through. But what you have just done is a very good thing! We're going to investigate to make sure it's all true. However, since you brought this information forward yourself, we're going to release you on your own recognizance. We don't see you as a threat or a flight risk."

Eventually, the police called him in and processed him through booking. Again, they let him out on his own recognizance. He stayed at the Mission, where he met some pastors who really helped him. They became like his mom and dad. They encouraged and loved him during the two weeks before he went to prison.

Then there was the court case and the sentencing: "This court finds you guilty on all counts. You are sentenced to 78 months incarceration."

"God, this is more than I can bear!" Sam groaned.

In an instant, Sam's heart was flooded with peace. The prosecutor took him upstairs to sign various documents. As he went with her, he found himself filled with concern for her. He knew somehow that she had pursued a Christian life at one time, but had become disillusioned. He shared his testimony with her and she responded with tears. Then Sam looked her in the eyes, and said to her,

"Do you want to see a miracle of God?"

"I could really use one right now," she said.

"Follow my life. I don't really understand what God has done, but I know He has done something wonderful. Follow my life, and you will see a miracle of God!"

REAL LIFE IN PRISON

Sam was scared in prison—so scared he thought he might die from fear. The fear was so thick in prison that it actually had a smell. But Sam was on a training ground, and God began to show him that He would protect and use him there.

Sam's cell became a place where guys who had been in prison for many years could come and pour out their hearts. Many of them received the Lord. The official church inside the prison grew. Out of a prison population of 1,500, the church grew from six to 150 by the time Sam left, and is still growing today.

Only a limited number of prisoners—usually six—were legally allowed to gather in a cell, although occasionally the officers allowed more. The people who had become Christians met from cell to cell—literally a "cell church!" Up and down the tiers, little groups met. They broke bread together using cherry Kool-Aid and stale crackers. These times became very important to the inmates, and many people on Sam's tier experienced life change.

A man who had been a Wiccan high priest was one of the new converts. (Wicca is a pagan religion that teaches the worship of various goddesses and gods and the practice of magical arts.) As a priest, he was accustomed to praying and fasting three times a week. Jim became a brother in Christ and one of the most successful soul winners in the penitentiary. They had many beautiful experiences together. Three prison riots were stopped with prayer. Whenever they heard a riot was being organized, three of them sat in the middle of the prison yard and prayed. God brought peace, and things quickly returned to normal.

Another time, Jim came over to Sam.

"We have to go clean the house. Stay here a minute!" Then Jim was gone. He returned with a piece of paper that granted them permission to go to the chapel an hour before each service to set up chairs and pray over the building.

As soon as they walked into the chapel, Jim dropped to his knees and started crying out to God.

"Lord, cleanse this house! We repent for what has gone on here. Please come and cleanse this house."

They prayed over everything—the doors, the chairs, the altar, the music equipment.

Two weeks later, the prison chaplain came up to them with a puzzled look on his face.

"Do you know what's just happened?" he asked.

"No. What?"

"The Wiccans and the Native Americans who practice their tribal religions just visited me. They said I need to get them a different building to meet in. When I asked them why, they said, 'There's something wrong in this place. "...We can't raise our spirits here any more!'"

Throughout his six years in prison, Sam documented his journey by creating songs and poems about what God was doing, and he continued writing after his release. He went back to the Mission, and went through a two-year Life Regeneration Discipleship program.

Church life outside the prison was frustrating for Sam. In prison, men have no reason to hide what has happened to them; everything they've done has been on radio or TV or in the newspaper. With nothing to hide, people are very real and don't try to cover up their problems. When he went to various churches, Sam found, with a few exceptions, people there were not real. They were hiding behind masks. It seemed their God was dead, because the people only talked about what God did six or ten years ago, as though that was the highlight of His activities.

"Did God die? God moves every day. Why aren't these people experiencing Him now?" he asked himself.

Sam found himself wanting to go back to prison where God was real. It was a fierce and difficult battle.

CANDY BAR EVANGELISM

When Sam finished the Mission program, he knew he had to do something different or he would end up back in prison. So he and a couple of others started an outreach at a local restaurant. They called it S.C.U.M.—Simple Christians Under Maintenance. People from the streets were involved, and they were as real as those in prison had been. God started moving immediately.

One day, Sam went with a friend to visit a cemetery. (He didn't have his own car and he had to get rides from other people.) The friend, Jenny, stopped to put flowers on her uncle's grave. While he was waiting for her, Sam saw a nice grassy area. He and Jenny walked down the hill towards it.

"I think this would be a perfect area for a SCUM outreach," Jenny commented. (SCUM was outgrowing the restaurant by this stage.) As they looked around them, they noticed some makeshift huts and a couple under a blanket.

"Oh, no! This is People's Park," exclaimed Jenny. People's Park is a nudist colony where anything goes. Some sections are peaceful, but drugs, sex, homosexuality and witchcraft run rampant in other areas. Murders even happen there.

Sam and Jenny high-tailed it out of there as quickly as they could. But when they got to the car, they both instantly started weeping. They realized that, in their hearts, they had judged the people living there.

"What can we do that would make a difference here," they wondered.

Jenny and Sam made some "friendship candy bars." Sam wrote poems and Jenny illustrated them and put scriptures onto labels and taped them around some Hershey's candy bars. He and Jenny took a bucket of these down to People's Park with some ice and some more poems in plastic sleeves and left them there.

As they reached the outskirts of the park on their way out, they were praying.

"Look!" said Jenny suddenly, elbowing Sam in the ribs.

A snake, two inches in diameter, was slithering across his feet.

"We've asked God to show us the strongholds in this city. I believe God is showing us that People's Park is one of them," Jenny and Sam agreed.

Together they prayed and claimed the area for Jesus Christ.

About one month later, Sam was sitting at a table in a restaurant, writing. A guy came in and approached him.

"You look like a Christian. Can I talk to you?" he asked.

Sam wondered what made him look like a Christian. It wasn't as if he had a Bible on the table or was wearing a T-shirt that identified him.

"Sure, sit down. You look hungry. Let me get you something to eat."

Jeff started telling his story.

"My parents are ministers, and all my life they have talked to me about Jesus. They would get frustrated with me because I couldn't accept Christianity. The other night, I couldn't sleep, and so I went out walking. I walked for several hours, and I kept telling God, 'If You are really there like my parents say You are, and if You really love me the way they say You do, I need a miracle!' On my way back—you're not going to believe this—I found this bucket filled with candy bars with labels on them talking about friendship with God and how much He loves me."

Sam prayed with Jeff to receive the Lord that day. Three weeks later, Jeff came back to the restaurant with several of his friends. Sam was there.

"No way! This is the dude I was telling you about!" Jeff exclaimed to his friends.

They all crowded into the booth with him.

"What's that?" Jeff asked, looking at the book of poems Sam had open on the table. He looked at the book. Then he looked at Sam and his eyes got big as he read the name of the author, and the realization suddenly hit him.

"No way! That was you?" He started crying and told his friends, "This is the dude that wrote that stuff!"

His friends were so blown away that all but one received the Lord that day.

FELONY FLATS

Eventually Sam moved from the Mission into an apartment within a house. He knew he had to do something in the drug-infested streets surrounding him. So he and a couple of others started a Bible study at his apartment with people from the streets. The numbers climbed, from seven to 12, and then from 12 to 20, and then from 20 to 45. By this stage there was no more room in his home, so he moved the meeting outside. Overnight, 90-plus people met in his front yard!

Some Christians from other churches attended. They said things to him such as, "Sam, I'm hoping that by coming down here I'm going to learn how to love my family." It was as though they learned more in the reality of life with people from the streets than in their own churches. Incredible miracles happened. Food was multiplied, people were healed and delivered and many were set free!

Sam and Jenny called the group "Off-Broadway"—partly because the apartment was on a street called Broadway, and partly because they helped people off the broad way and onto the narrow way with Jesus.

Before long, Sam was called into a meeting with some of the servant leaders of the city. This group, the most influential pastors of the area, was considering Sam for the position of prayer coordinator for his section of the city. They wanted to know where he was coming from and what he was doing. He told them everything—including all the junk.

"I have no training except for what I learned in prison. I was tested and challenged there on everything I believe. I have no degrees. I know what it's like to walk in darkness, and I believe God wants to use me to help people make the transition into His Kingdom of light."

For a few short minutes, you could hear a pin drop. Then one man stood up.

"Sam, I wish we had a hundred more men just like you!"

The group of pastors rose to their feet. They surrounded Sam, laid hands on him, anointed him with oil and said, "Go! Do not look for work any longer; you are doing what God has called you to do!" That was an incredible experience for Sam. He knew from that day on he was anointed by God for ministry.

Sam cried all the way back to his house because of the sense of anointing that was confirmed by the laying on of hands. Since that day, he has felt empowered for ministry, even though he knows God used him before this happened.

God continued to move in miraculous ways. A man he knew, who also was active in ministry to others, bought a couple of houses a few blocks from his apartment. Sam moved into that house with a few others.

During the time he lived in the apartment, the whole neighborhood changed. Within one year, all the drug houses moved from the neighborhood. Still, in his heart, Sam did not want them to move out; he wanted them to change!

Both of the areas where Sam lived were known as "Felony Flats" because so many felons were released to that area. There were several drug houses, and more felonies were committed there than other areas of the city. Right away, Sam and his friends started going into his neighbors' homes and getting to know people. In the new location, God moved again. Soon, the front yard of this house was filled with between 200 and 250 people.

At the beginning, many volunteers from other churches came to help. Some of them brought "in-a-box thinking" (limiting how God is "allowed" to act), and almost destroyed what God was doing. At times, Sam even found himself caught up in the same way of thinking. But God is faithful, and He continued to move until Sam and his friends finally realized what was happening.

One man, Bill, stuck with him. Bill was concerned that he didn't fit in with the people from the area. That was true; Bill did not fit in. But because he stayed and stuck things out, the people grew to accept him. He and Sam began to go into the drug houses, and befriended the people together.

Five major drug houses on Sam's street were attached to three drug "cartels." Now only one drug house is there, and it is unattached to any of the cartels. Although one moved away, the others have not. Instead, they have changed!

For more than 20 years, people from different churches have prayer-walked these streets. Sam is convinced what he is seeing happen is a result of their prayers. They planted and watered, and now it is harvest time!

TRANSFORMATIONS

One evening, one of the people who regularly prayer-walks called them.

"I want to get a group together to pray over the drug house just around the corner from you," he said.

Sam and his friends agreed because they didn't want to dampen their friend's faith, but they were merely humoring him. A group of them met to pray over the drug house on a Thursday evening around 10:00 P.M., when there is a lot of activity around the house. As people were going in and out to buy drugs, they had to pass through the group of praying believers to get to the house, because they stood only six feet or so from the door. Sam could tell that people didn't know how to react to them; they looked visibly shaken!

All of a sudden, the Holy Spirit moved. Without really knowing why, the group started to sing.

"Amazing grace, how sweet the sound,
   That saved a wretch like me..."

The sweet melody wafted through the evening air. Soon the lights in the drug house were turned off—business was shut down for the night. The group returned home.

The next day, Sam's friend who instigated prayer the night before visited neighbors of the drug house that had been prayed over. The lady who ran the drug house came out as they were standing on the street, and told them some of her story.

The parents of this lady were pastors, and she was raised in church. When both her parents died at an early age, she blamed God for taking them and went on a rebellious streak.

"I'm stuck now. I don't have a choice. I'm in too far," Nancy told them. "But you know, last night, when you guys started singing that song "Amazing Grace," I couldn't control myself. I sat on my couch and I just wept. I cried and cried, and nobody could get me to do anything. So they turned the light off and shut down for the night."

A few weeks later, there was a knock on Sam's door. When he

answered it, Nancy was standing there.

"I wanted you to know I've left all that stuff," she told them. "The drugs, the money, everything. I've left it all behind. And now I'm about to turn myself in! I'm not too worried about being locked up because I'm no longer locked up here," as she pointed to her heart. She looked up with a huge smile Sam easily recognized.

"Nancy, could I give you a hug?"

"I'd really like that."

Sam gave her a big hug, and then he looked over at her.

"We'll walk with you! We'll walk with you! Keep in contact with us because we'll walk through this with you. Jesus loves you!" Nancy just wept. It is one of most beautiful things that ever happened to Sam.

Two hours after Nancy left to turn herself in, the police raided her house with a warrant for her arrest.

The church there is in transition. They want to keep the big meeting on Monday nights where people can visit Sam's house for the food, music and fellowship. The rest of the week, they will meet in groups in homes. But they want to start groups in the drug houses as people there find the Lord. Some of the people who will go to a meeting in a drug house would never visit Sam's home. They are ready to start in at least three different houses. Sam plans to get the church started, and then pull out quickly so they are on their own. That way they won't develop a dependency on outsiders, but will have to rely on the Holy Spirit.

Ben, Sam's son who became addicted to methamphetamines, is also a victory story. One evening while Sam was taking care of two heroin addicts, there was a knock at the door. When Sam opened it, three of the upper-level drug dealers were standing there.

"We want you to come with us," they said.

Sam was concerned, but felt a gentle nudge from the Holy Spirit that he should go with them. They drove to an abandoned parking lot.

"Ben comes to us for drugs," they told him. "But we've seen the way you care for people in our area, and we want to let you know that we are refusing to supply him any more. If he wants to get drugs, he'll have to go elsewhere."

For a while, Ben was clean. But then he had a relapse and bought drugs in a different area. Then he started acting confused.

So Sam took Ben away with him for nine days to an out-of-town ranch. God gave Sam his son back. Ben met with God, and people are amazed at the difference in him. They tell Ben that he has a light in him now that they've never seen in him before.

Many lives in Sam's neighborhood have changed; Sam figures that at least 300 people have been touched by what God is doing. To outsiders, things might still seem bad; for example, the new believers still use a lot of profanity.

"Can you imagine how bad their language was before?" Sam says. "Some people might look at these men and say, 'That's not what a Christian looks like,' but I have lived with these men. I know them, and the changes are profound.

"One time I went to the hospital with Chris, one of the major drug dealers who had just become a Christian, to see his girlfriend. The girlfriend was given a shot of morphine, and the nurse left a syringe that still contained some liquid. As soon as Chris saw it, he started shaking. I put myself between Chris and the syringe so he could no longer see it. But as we were leaving, Chris picked up the syringe and put it in his pocket. I looked at Chris, shook my head and said 'No!' Chris then handed the syringe to the nurse.

'You'd better do something with this before someone else takes it,' Chris said.

"That is where the battles are for these people. They are not going to look like Christians to some people, but the changes in their lives are incredible.

"I love these people. People on the streets are so real. A man will say to me, 'Do you mind if I bring my boyfriend?' We don't have to hide from the truth of what God's Word says, but we don't have to shun them. Because of that, they are very open with us. I'll ask some people, 'Have you used? What's your drug of choice? If you like, we will help you. We cannot, but Jesus can. We can lead you to Him and show you how you can live a life that will be more fulfilling.' I am hooked on this kind of living!

"One day I had a vision that I was walking down the street holding onto God's pant leg. He had his arm around me. We're walking and He's doing all this amazing stuff, healing the sick, bringing deliverance, performing miracles, and setting all these people free. And as we go along, He pats me on the head and says, 'Nice job, son.' We get to the end of the block and I cannot take it any more. I say, 'But Lord, you did this stuff, not me!' And He says, 'Yes I know, but we're a team!'"

KEY THOUGHTS: "GOOD SOIL"

Jesus tells us that the fields are ripe and ready to harvest. (John 4:35) Why are we not seeing more fruit in the church today? Could it be that we are trying to bring in a harvest from fields that are not yet ripe?

In the parable of the sower, Jesus describes four different kinds of soil, only one of which produces a plentiful harvest. (Matthew 13:3-23) What makes a person into good soil? Neil Cole of Greenhouse has a graphic way of putting it. He says, "Bad people make good soil because they have plenty of 'fertilizer' in their lives."

One of the names given to Jesus is "friend of sinners." Not many of our Christian songs are written on this aspect of His character. But Jesus was renowned for hanging around tax collectors and sinners. (Matthew 11:19) He ate and drank with them and attended their parties. (Mark 2:15-17; Luke 5:27-32) He didn't flinch when a prostitute anointed His feet with perfume. (Luke 7:36-50) But we are often so scared of being contaminated by sin that we won't go to the places where these people are to be found. Or maybe we're concerned that someone will see us there and get the wrong impression!

If we stay in nice middle-class neighborhoods, we are not nearly as likely to see a bountiful harvest of souls as if we go to the gutters, to the places where people know they have a need. We're far more likely to find people receptive to the gospel if we go to the poor, or to those with problems. How about getting involved in a 12-step program? Or maybe ask the police where the problem areas are in your city. Or work with the homeless or those just out of jail.

We are also more likely to reap a harvest if we go to places where people are seeking spiritual answers. For example, I recently heard of a group of Christians that offers "dream interpretation" at spiritual festivals for New Age followers. This provides them with a ready access to people who are looking for spirituality.

Sam and the people he works with are "good soil." God is using them powerfully to reach many. Please pray for them.

DAVID'S STORY

"I will build My church"

HARRY POTTER AND TATTOOS

David has worked for a jewelry manufacturer for the past seven years as a maintenance supervisor. Twice each year, the entire plant shuts down to service all the equipment. He has two guys he works closely with in the department, and over the years they have become friends. They discuss all kinds of different topics together and much friendly banter passes between them.

"So what do you think about Harry Potter, David?" John asked one day as they were working on some of the equipment.

"I'm not sure you really want me to tell you what I think about that subject," David replied.

"Yes, go on!"

"I know what the Scriptures say about witchcraft, and that is more important than what I think. What I see is that God hates witchcraft. I know others might not agree with me, but I don't think it's right to make light of it," was David's reply. John and Harry sat and listened for half an hour while David explained his thoughts to them.

All the water in the manufacturing plant runs through large tanks where it is filtered to collect any particles of precious metals. Every six months, the filters are changed so that the gold can be refined from them. The next day, David was walking through the plant to perform this task. As he passed between the counters where the gems are counted and examined for flaws, John and Harry were there taking a break.

"So tell us what you think about tattoos, David?" John said, pointing to the tattoo on his upper arm.

"Tattoos show who you belong to, and where your identity is. I belong to my heavenly Father. I am marked with His name on my heart, so I don't need a tattoo. My identity comes from my Father through Jesus Christ. I am a son of God. Who do you belong to?"

Two hours of discussion later, David discovered that Harry attended a church but really had no idea about the things that he was hearing there. John was a committed member of the Church of the Latter Day Saints (LDS) who loved to ask questions.

"What if I came to your home and we studied the Bible and tried to find the answers to some of these things?" David asked as they ended their time together.

And that is how this simple church started. Four couples from David's work—only two with any meaningful relationship with God—gathered at one of their homes. Within a month or so, all had committed their lives to the Lord as they came to understand what Jesus had done for them.

One day at work, John chatted with another LDS lady who worked next to him, and shared some of the things he had been learning at his new church. David was working close by and every so often, John would fire a question at him to get his help. At the end of the afternoon, the lady came up to David.

"I know I've been taught wrong. Please, will you teach me?"

For a number of years, David has "ministered" at work. If any of the other employees have a need, whether it is their health, or in their family, they know David will pray for them. (Everyone at his work now knows that if David heads out to the garage with someone, they're going to pray together.) He pastors more at his job than in any of the traditional churches he has led.

A group of eight ladies from work that David "pastored" formed a new group with the lady who asked him for help; all of them have now become followers of Jesus.

As he makes disciples, David finds that Jesus is building His church. Five churches have formed from that company of 35 employees.

GOD WORKS LOCALLY

David was raised in a Pentecostal denomination. After he left Bible school, he worked as an assistant pastor in a small, rural church. When the senior pastor first told him that he would be responsible for the cell group ministry, he was horrified. His understanding of cell groups was that they caused rebellion. However, he soon found that God had given him an ability to get them started. Within his little church of around 100 people who attended on Sundays, he started 23 cells. (Not all the people who were in the cells came to the main church meetings.)

Nine years ago, David moved to his current small-town location at the request of his senior pastor, who wanted to encourage church growth. His job was to administer and oversee the cell group ministry. Despite David's best efforts, he couldn't get even one cell group started in this new situation, and eventually the work collapsed. But he had a conviction that he was supposed to be in that location.

So David and his wife, Vickie, launched out again on their own, still under the auspices of the original church. When he became part of a local pastors' prayer group, David realized he needed an attitude adjustment. The group of churches he belonged to thought they were right about everything, and David had to humble himself to this group of pastors. However, his new outlook on life alienated a lot of people in the leadership of his denomination. The church eventually left the denomination.

At this stage, around 40 people attended the church in a small storefront.

Over the next few months, several things changed David's understanding of church. First, a man named Robert Fitts spoke to the church. (Robert travels the country helping others with his 4H vision: House Churches, Healing Rooms, Home Bible Colleges and Houses of Prayer.) He spoke to them about the scriptural basis of church in the home. David was ready to apply some of what he heard, but certainly not all. It was much too radical!

Another local leader challenged them to learn to distinguish between true apostles and false apostles. A false apostle raises up people and then hoards them to build his own ministry. A true apostle raises up people and releases them to build the Kingdom of God.

A friend who ran a Bible book store began feeding David material about house church by Wolfgang Simson. (Wolfgang is a church growth specialist who has written extensively on house church. *Houses that Change the World* is perhaps the most influential book on the subject. People all over the world have read it and have started simple churches meeting in homes.) At first, David would say to him, "Stop it! What do I want with that stuff?" But as the ideas gradually took root in his mind, he experienced a paradigm shift in his thinking.

Then the Lord took away their church building, and they had to meet in homes. Originally they thought the Lord would provide another building. But now, with the expansion of groups from David's work, their vision is to start more and more churches wherever they can.

One of the guys in this church was an alcoholic who now is totally set free. He continues to go to weekly Alcoholics Anonymous meetings where he tells people about Jesus and His power to set them free. He leads them to pray to The Higher Power.

Another group gathers on an Indian reservation. A Native American lady started her own church there. But she had to move and asked David to lead it. Everything in that church is done from the mindset of family and simple church.

One day, as David was driving past a coffee shop, he sensed he needed to go inside. He discovered that the owners are Christians and they became friends. One of the groups now meets there on a Saturday morning. Six or seven of them get together and bring friends who aren't yet believers. Over coffee, they present Jesus Christ as the truth and the answer to life's questions.

In the past two years they have seen 13 different groups form that meet in homes, or in coffee shops. Every day before work begins at the jewelry company, the believers get together for Bible study and prayer with the encouragement of their employer.

How is all this happening? Let's ask David.

"The Lord is making this thing happen at a grass-roots level, person to person. We tell people that they are the seed of the Kingdom, and wherever the wind of the Holy Spirit blows them is where they're supposed to be. We suggest to people that they pray for a chance to speak to one person about Jesus. Then they walk with an opportunity mindset until the Lord opens a door. As soon as they see a door of opportunity open for a relationship, they walk through it. They are not trying to convert the person, but merely let the Lord create a friendship. They soon find that they can talk to them about Jesus. Then they suggest that they read Scripture together. Others soon join them. That's how disciples are being made and churches are multiplying locally."

Sometimes the churches come together for larger meetings. They didn't sit down and say, "Gee, let's have our big meetings in the park!" Out of necessity, with no building, they use different parks around the city. Over the past two years, park meetings have become one of the main ways they connect—not just in the city, but regionally as well. The Lord brings someone into town with a message for the churches, and a meeting is organized around their visit—sometimes in just a few days. In the past two years, people have come from many other countries, as well as from the United States. During the winter, when it's far too cold to meet outdoors, friends from traditional churches allow them to use their buildings.

GOD WORKS REGIONALLY

God is not only building His church at David's job or in his city. It's plain that He is also doing something remarkable on a regional basis. Through a series of relationships across an area of several hundred square miles, from city to city, God is creating a network of friendships.

This is how David describes it:

"I have a vision of a net stretching across the region. The knots signify relationships. The net is designed to bring in the harvest. At the moment, the Lord is not drawing in the net because it would break. But as it grows stronger, He will start to use it.

"Everything comes first in a seed package; the end result will look different from the beginning. Sometimes when I meet someone, the Lord will put it into my heart that this is important, and I will take their name. And the Lord is building strategic relationships with some of those people.

"For example, near the original church where I was associate pastor many years ago, a church was going through renewal. I used to make fun of them and call them the 'Church of the Weird!' Then when I moved here, I met them. And I had to confess my attitude to them and repent with tears. Later, while we were visiting with them in their small city, they introduced us to some people from another city. We fell in love with each other, out there in the middle of nowhere. Over the course of time, we have both started house churches. They have three or four groups in their city.

"On another occasion someone called our home by mistake, and we found out about two simple churches we didn't know existed in a neighboring city. Dynamic leaders led them, and they were bursting out of their homes. We put them in touch with each other, and helped them see that they need to multiply. Now they work together and have joint meetings. They have groups full of people of substance who could easily be doing what they do. So we challenged them to encourage people to look for opportunities in their homes and on their jobs to start reproducing the family. Now they are sending people out to start new groups.

"God is putting together a network of relationships of people with similar regional vision. We are beginning to work together. We had a meeting recently with people from eight different cities separated by more than 450 miles. We watched knots being tied. Now we're working together all the time. And all of these relationships happened through amazing divine coincidences.

"I believe the Lord is preparing this net for the final harvest. We tell people again and again that they are the seed of the Kingdom. The Spirit blows where He wills, and He knows where He is sending them. Wherever they end up, they need to land with their eyes wide open to see what God is doing. And then they join Him in it. We're looking to raise spiritual sons, who become fathers, who can in turn raise sons. We want to see the Kingdom reproduced through these family relationships. And we are finding that He is leading us to the right places and He is tying the knots.

"We're looking to be led by the Lord, not just following a ritual or formula. We don't only want to do what we see in the New Testament. We want to see why they did what they did. We don't want to miss planting the seed that produces fruit. God is doing something unique in each area and we want to find it, not just follow someone else's pattern.

"He is orchestrating a collection of relationships. We didn't sit down and try to figure it out. We are watching the Lord do something dynamic and special, created in His mind not ours. Jesus is building His church!"

KEY THOUGHTS: "I WILL BUILD MY CHURCH"

Church is not about buildings or meetings; it's not about church structure or charismatic leaders. Church is about relationships, first with Jesus and then with those in His body. Jesus needs to be our primary focus—pleasing Him our highest calling, communicating with Him the heartbeat of our existence. If we are in love with Jesus above all else, not only individually but corporately, then our expressions of church are likely to be healthy and vibrant.

In Ephesians 4:14-15, Jesus is described as the head of His church. In Matthew 16:18, Jesus states, "I will build My church."

Too often, Jesus is head of His church in name only. We call Him, "Lord, Lord," but actually give Him no real power to impact what happens in His body. (Matthew 7:21) We don't consult Him on decisions, even though they are made in His name. He is like a constitutional monarch, such as we have in England. Even though a lot of pomp and show revolve around the Queen, the authority actually rests in Parliament. The Queen is virtually powerless.

A. W. Tozer wrote, "The God of the modern evangelical rarely astonishes anybody. He manages to stay pretty much within the constitution. Never breaks our bylaws. He's a very well-behaved God and very denominational and very much one of us, and we ask Him to help us when we're in trouble and look to Him to watch over us when we're asleep. The God of the modern evangelical isn't a God I could have much respect for. But when the Holy Ghost shows us God as He is, we admire Him to the point of wonder and delight." (*Worship: The Missing Jewel of the Evangelical Church*)

We have relegated Jesus to a place of impotence. We create our own blueprint for what we want Him to do, asking His blessing on our programs and building things the way we think is best according to the latest and greatest church growth statistics. We do not even pause to think that Jesus might have a master-design. If we were to each individually or as churches follow His plan for our situation, the Holy Spirit would orchestrate something way beyond anything we could ask or imagine.

In a recent issue of *Catch the Fire* magazine, John Arnott states, "Seemingly, the Holy Spirit has no problem coordinating hundreds and thousands of different individuals and congregations for His eternal purposes. Things really do work much better when Jesus Himself is the head."

Let's give God His church back! Enough of our programs and plans! It's all about Jesus! Jesus is the Head. We, the Church, are His body. Let's fall in love with Jesus all over again, and seek God for His will for us as individuals, and corporately for our churches.

What David describes in this story is exciting because it is a practical outworking of this on a small scale. God is creating a network of relationships that He is using to build His church in that region.

Jesus as head of His church is a foundational principle for simple churches. Jesus, build Your church!

LISA'S
STORY

Church is built on relationships

A SEARCH FOR INTIMACY AND SPIRITUALITY

*(**Be warned.** Lisa's story is unusual, and may challenge your preconceived notions of how God is allowed to work. Like Cornelius, she was touched by the Holy Spirit before she had a relationship with the Lord. And He used a New Age therapist's couch as the place to meet her! God has had His hand on Lisa and He has moved in unconventional ways to transform her life. God cannot be confined to our theological boxes. As C.S. Lewis says, "Aslan is not a tame lion!")*

"Honey, I know this is weird, but I met this guy on an Internet site," Lisa told her husband, Kurtis. (These have to be among the last words a loving husband wants to hear from his wife!)

"He's talking this Christian lingo about intimacy and spirituality, and the stuff he writes is amazing. I feel that I'm supposed to be talking with him and that we were put together by God!"

"Well, it is a little weird," Kurtis replied, "and I'm not really sure how I feel about it. But yeah, it's OK for you to correspond with him." (Kurtis is a very unusual guy!)

Here's how Lisa's story begins...

Lisa has been searching for something more in her life ever since she can remember. She tried to find fulfillment through deeper relationships with family members, but that wasn't something that came naturally to them. Her desire for intimacy and relationship led her to try many different things to fill the emptiness inside. But drugs, alcohol and sex failed to fill that void.

At the age of 21, Lisa became a Christian. A friend led her to

Christ, and for a while she went to church. At the time, she was living at home with her mother, but it wasn't a good situation. Her mother spent most of each day locked in her room, depressed because her husband had left her. Lisa worked full time and was taking a full load at school. The lack of sleep, along with her home situation, resulted in her emotional instability. The people who led her to Christ were young Christians themselves, and didn't know how to deal with all Lisa was going through.

Her experience at church was not good, either. She didn't feel she could connect with anybody there. One day, on the church grounds, she was so distraught with the problems in her life that she sat on the ground crying. Some church leaders walked by her as she sat there. They totally ignored her and didn't even try to reach out and help her!

Lisa was dating Kurtis, a wonderful man, tall and good-looking; he loved her and wanted to marry her. But he did not want to deal with her Christianity. Lisa loved Kurtis, and desperately wanted and needed the stability that he represented. So she put Christianity on the back burner.

Lisa and Kurtis went through many years of counseling together, including a period of time when Lisa took antidepressants. Though her marriage was good, she still didn't have the intimacy she longed for, and eventually resigned herself to the fact that life was going to be like this.

Thanks to a hysterectomy, Lisa woke up to the fact that it was time to heal. After trying many methods, Lisa decided to see a therapist who did some kind of strange energy work.

Just before her third session with Dave, the energy therapist, Lisa sensed something significant was about to happen. So she prayed before she went in.

"Jesus, will You and God and the angels be there with me? May I know Your love, and please will You heal me?"

Dave did something more unusual this time. As Lisa was lying on the table, Dave shook rattles over her, and told her to let go and fall. She felt as though she was falling through the table, and had a sense of high-frequency vibrations throughout her body.

When Lisa got off the table, she was a changed person. The

physical sensations were so intense she wasn't sure if she could make it home. They lasted for about three days, but the feelings of peace and joy, aliveness and overflowing love were permanent. Simultaneously, she felt a deepened desire for intimacy. At the time, she didn't know how to account for the change. But she remembered asking God to be there and to heal her. So she had a strong conviction that somehow it was God.

Dave also told her, "I have the impression that you are going to meet a man in the future who will change your life. You will be so changed that you will have no words for it—the words won't even be in your vocabulary. And it's going to be soon!"

LISA AND JAY

Around this time, another friend recommended to Lisa some books on spirituality and sexuality. They did not advocate any particular religion, but definitely had an Eastern flavor. Impressed with their content, Lisa visited the author's website and discovered a bulletin board. Again, she had an intuition that she was supposed to write something on the list. So even though it went against her natural inclination, she started posting on the board.

When she checked her private email the day after she made her second posting on the site, a man named Jay responded to her post. A couple of things caught her attention.

"Our greatest desire is for intimacy, and our greatest fear is of rejection," Jay wrote.

"We have to have other people in order to share love. We cannot do it on our own—there has to be someone else to experience it with."

This was music to Lisa's ears.

Jay went on to talk about four different kinds of love. He quoted C.S. Lewis. He talked about Jesus being a garbage man who could deal with the garbage in our lives.

Lisa's first inclination was to ignore it. Her previous experience with church had not been that positive, and she was worried about having to go through the Christianity thing with Kurtis again. Although he had a church background, Kurtis had quit Christianity because it was too restrictive and had too many rules. It didn't feel alive to him. Here was Lisa, feeling extremely enlivened and wanting to improve her relationship with Kurtis, and she was concerned that Christian doctrine would be too narrow and limiting.

But she remembered Dave's word to her about meeting a man who would change her life, so she asked Kurtis if he would mind her corresponding with Jay.

That December, Lisa and Jay started an email conversation. Two months later, the New Age bulletin board went away!

The email exchange between Jay and Lisa was based on the Bible. Jay sent Bible quotes, and Lisa looked up the references and emailed him back with any questions.

One of the first things Jay did was to apologize to Lisa.

"I cannot proceed further without first asking your forgiveness for what may have been represented to you as 'church.'"

Jay also talked to her about church in the home.

"In the New Testament, that was the way church used to be. It's a pattern for us today."

Jay is a committed Christian. He arrived at the same web list as Lisa because a friend was given a CD on spiritual intimacy, and Jay was concerned for them.

The spiritual bond grew over the months between Jay and Lisa. It was very apparent that the Lord had put them together, and that Lisa was being fed at a deep, spiritual level. She discovered Jay had been a Christian for more than 30 years. She always had a great respect for her elders, and had never heard a Christian talk this way before. He never tried to squelch any of her experiences, or make her feel different or "bad." It was an amazing experience for her and it wasn't long before Lisa began to regard Jay as a "spiritual father." She also began to learn a new vocabulary, just as Dave had predicted.

Lisa knew about being "born again" from her previous experience with Christianity. Through emailing Jay, she learned about the Holy Spirit, and remembered her experience in Dave's consulting room.

"Whoa, do you think that could have been the Holy Spirit?" she thought, and emailed asking Jay.

He wrote back to her describing the whole concept of "prevenience," where God is at work in our lives even before we really know Him.

"Judging by the fruit in your life, I believe this could have been the Holy Spirit!"

Lisa was concerned because she didn't have a more conventional experience.

"God, if that experience on Dave's table was not from you, would you please take it away?" Lisa prayed.

On January 7th, Jay emailed her.

"Has your understanding reached the point of acknowledging that you belong to Jesus?"

To which Lisa replied, "I would have to go with my heart and say YES!!! I'm just sitting here now, feeling a sense of celebration taking place inside me. It's amazing!"

Lisa wanted to meet some Christians in her city, and wondered where she could go to church. She immediately thought of the Church of Faith and Serenity, a New Age church where some close friends attended.

Jay, realizing her need for fellowship where she lived, scrambled to find someone or locate a group near Lisa. Jay remembered an Internet database, and came across a telephone number in her city with no name attached to it. When he called the number, he found himself talking with Tony, who was leading a network of home churches in that city! Jay and his wife, Carleen, met Tony two years before that at a house church conference.

"I think you will find that Tony and his wife are a lifesaver for you," Jay told her.

Jay put Lisa and Tony in touch, and it was only a matter of days before Kurtis and Lisa were sitting down at a Starbucks with Tony and his wife, a couple in their early 50s.

"CAN I HAVE CHURCH AT MY HOUSE?"

As Lisa and Kurtis told their stories, Lisa described how they had met weekly for 10 years with a group of friends to share about spirituality and strengthening their marriages. Tony made a suggestion.

"If you want to get some of your friends together, we can come to your house and meet with you to discuss spirituality."

In Lisa's experience, when a group of her friends came together, the girls would talk about spiritual things while the guys talked cars or sports. She thought it would be wonderful if the whole group explored spirituality together. After all, the only thing she wanted to talk about these days was Jesus. She thought it would be incredible if a group of people could connect on a regular basis, and at an intimate level discuss things of the Spirit and build each other up in love.

So within a few days, Lisa sent Tony an email.

"I would like to have church at my house," it said.

"I'll be there for you, but don't have any expectations from me. I'll just be there," was Kurtis' response to the idea.

As she met people over the next few days, Lisa would ask the Lord, "Is this someone I should ask to come?" If she heard "Yes," she would invite them to her home. In fact, she mentioned it to just about everyone she met, and several committed to come. Prior to this, Lisa never felt she had anything in her life worth sharing. But now she couldn't stop talking about what God was doing. Many were curious to come. Having known Lisa before, they could see the changes in her life; a few with religious backgrounds were put off by the fact that this was Christianity.

About a dozen people, mostly from Christian-turned-New Age backgrounds, gathered in Lisa's living room that first week. After a potluck meal, Tony asked each person to share.

"Tell the story of where you are on your spiritual journey."

Each person talked for several minutes about where their lives were at a spiritual level, and about the journey that had led them there. It was a deep and meaningful time, and several people committed to return the following week to take things further. Tony promised them he would have a spiritual book they could look at together and use as the basis of their discussions. They also broke into pairs and prayed for each other.

The next week they shared a meal together again.

"What 'God events' happened in anyone's life this week?" asked Tony. Everyone seemed to have something that happened that week they could attribute to God, and they shared what was going on in their lives.

"The book that I want us to look at together is the Gospel of John," Tony explained. "It comes from the Bible, which is the number one book of all time on spirituality.

"We are going to look at a passage in this way. We will use three symbols to help us: a question mark if there is something you do not understand, a candlestick if the passage sheds light on something going on in your life or something you are reading and an arrow if you sense God piercing your heart with something He wants to say to you."

They started their studies in the Gospel of John, taking it a verse or thought at a time. For that group, it was a wonderful introduction to Christianity, talking about light and life and other concepts that were comfortable for them to discuss. Tony did not explain the passage to them, but let them explore it together. There were no right or wrong answers, and everyone's opinion mattered. But he continually pointed them to the Scriptures as their authority.

Following the Bible discussion, they prayed for each other.

It took about four weeks for the group to accept the Bible as their authority. On the sixth week the group reached John 1:12, "To as many as received Him, to them He gave power to become the sons of God..."

"What does it mean to receive Him?" asked Sandy, a massage client of Lisa's who was involved in the group almost from the start with her boyfriend.

"I think to 'receive' means to commit," shared Traci, a single mom.

After some general discussion, everyone came to the conclusion that this was indeed a good definition.

Pat, a friend Lisa knew from singing in a choir, commented, "Commitment is a serious matter. It's like marriage."

"Why don't we each go to a different part of the house on our own, and commit our lives to Jesus?" suggested Tony. "Becoming a Christian can be as simple as committing as much as we know of ourselves to as much as we understand of God."

So each person went away for some personal time with God. When they came back, most had obviously had some kind of spiritual experience—there were lots of tears and hugs.

The group has grown much closer over time. Each of them, including Kurtis, is on the journey of discipleship. Tony and his wife pulled out after a few months once the group was functioning well. Lisa facilitates, under the Holy Spirit's guidance, with another long-standing Christian couple providing oversight. Jay continues to disciple Lisa by email. She has grown, in less than a year, into a remarkably mature Christian.

Lisa loves meeting with her friends and experiencing the presence of the Holy Spirit together with them. Through the Lord and those He puts in her life, she has found the love and intimacy she has desired for so long.

KEY THOUGHTS: CHURCH IS BUILT
ON RELATIONSHIPS

We have a friend who used to be the pastor of a legacy church in Denver. He tried an experiment. One afternoon, he sat at a coffee shop with a sign that read "I'll buy you a cup of coffee if you let me tell you my story about God." Only one person took him up on his offer. The next day he went to a different coffee shop. This time his sign read, "I'll buy you a cup of coffee if you tell me your story about God." This time people were lining up to spend time with him. Many of them ended up in tears. Most would refuse to let him buy them coffee, just thanking him profusely for listening to them.

Stories are powerful (hence the idea of this book!) People love to tell their stories. And they are often a good way to get to a person's heart. When we get a group of unbelievers together for the first time, we usually open things up by having each one tell us their story—where they are on their spiritual journey. It gives us a very good idea about their spiritual background and beliefs in a non-threatening way.

It's also important for us to learn how to tell our own story in a way that doesn't use Christian language, so that it is understandable to the not-yet believer. As we develop this skill, it becomes a tool that we use in multiple situations.

Stories also build relationships. When we know someone's story, we feel empathy and closeness with them. So our first gathering with a group of unbelievers usually contains this element, because we are aiming to build a spiritual community founded on relationships.

We base what happens in subsequent gatherings on Acts 2:42, where the disciples came together for "the apostles' doctrine and fellowship, for breaking of bread and for prayer." We share a meal together, we share what is going on in our lives, we study the Word, and we pray for one another.

We use this basic outline for all our times together, whether it is with unbelievers or mature believers. Some weeks we may find that the Holy Spirit emphasizes one area. For example, we may spend so much time praying for a situation that we do not have time to get into the Word. But in general, each of these areas is covered.

Lisa is a remarkable person. She radiates love and warmth, and delights in close and intimate friendships. Because of the way that she and Kurtis care for people, everyone who walks in the door of their home feels loved.

Church is meant to be community—vibrant and loving relationships, caring and sharing lives together. People are hungry for the Life that this represents. In John 13:35, Jesus says that when people see our love for each other, they will know that we are His disciples. Close and loving relationships are foundational to the DNA of organic, simple churches.

Our love for one another can be expressed in practical ways. Church was never meant to be a social club. There are over 50 "one another's" in the New Testament—instructions to love one another (John 13:34; Romans 13:8), serve one another (Galatians 5:13), bear one another's burdens (Galatians 6:2), teach and admonish one another (Colossians 3:16), etc. We need to be in a context where we can obey these commands. A small and close-knit community cultivates an atmosphere where this is natural.

Lisa is an example of how rapidly a person can grow in the Lord. Her mentoring relationship with Jay has fostered a hunger for the things of God and this has produced a remarkably mature Christian in a very short time.

But Lisa's story also illustrates another principle. The resources for the harvest are in the harvest. When someone becomes a Christian, it can often be more effective to have them start something within their circle of relationships. Lisa is a person of peace. She quickly opened up her sphere of influence for the gospel. Right from the start, Lisa was the one who facilitated the group. It did not require someone who had been a Christian for years. With help from more mature Christians, Lisa has been an effective laborer in her harvest field.

Lisa and Jay have written a book based on their email correspondence. For more information, see their website at www.notleftbehind.net.

THOMAS & MARIE'S STORY

Church is family

FAMILY CHURCH

Thomas and Marie have a wonderful family. Their two children, Joy and Stephen, love learning about the Lord. But it hasn't always been so exciting.

Seven years ago, Thomas and Marie were attending a mega-church. It was a great church with good programs, and they had been members for several years. Every Sunday, Joy (then age eight) and Stephen (age six) went to their own classes during the sermon.

One day, on the way home from church, Joy made an announcement: "Mom, Dad, if I hear one more story about Noah and the ark in Sunday School, I'm going to throw up."

So Marie and Thomas began to pray. Shortly after this, the family moved out to the country, about 45 minutes away from the city and their church.

Thomas works for a ministry which has the goal of seeing a church within walking distance of every person worldwide. He was very familiar with the fact that, in many other parts of the world such as India and China, the church is exploding with growth because of church planting movements. (A church planting movement is a rapid multiplication of churches led by non-professional local people within their own culture. This is mainly accomplished through house churches). He had read books by people such as Robert Fitts about simple churches in homes being relevant in a Western culture. As he and Marie discussed and prayed about what to do about church, they concluded that, since they were home schooling their children, a house church might be best for their family.

Thomas didn't want to do anything without the blessing of his pastor. So he went to the pastor and asked if he would validate the idea of planting a church in their new home.

"I really want your blessing," Thomas told him. The pastor was very encouraging.

"Kneel down," the pastor suggested. He laid his hands on Thomas and prayed, "Lord, I know Thomas, and I trust Thomas. I know that he's Your son and You're calling him to lead a gathering. So I'm going to release him, in Jesus' Name, to do this."

Following breakfast on the first Sunday morning in their new home, Thomas sat his kids down on the couch in the living room. He stood in front of them, Bible held out, just like a preacher in a mega-church. "Now kids, I want you to turn to 1 Kings, chapter 1." Thomas taught the Scriptures, verse by verse, sharing and interacting with his family...for four hours!

As the weeks went by, they covered 1 and 2 Kings and 1 and 2 Samuel. And the kids loved it! At first, Thomas thought it was his teaching they enjoyed. Later he came to realize that it was actually their dad spending the whole day with them that they loved!

This insight caused Thomas to re-evaluate his understanding of church. As he went through this process, he increasingly recognized that it was as valuable for him to listen to his kids as it was to teach them. The kids loved to enter into discussions about the passages Thomas shared, and they memorized huge passages of Scripture. They were really excited about church at home.

There was something else the family did initially that was different. Week by week, they kneeled or sat on the floor, held hands and asked the Holy Spirit to come and visit them. Sometimes they would stay there for up to half an hour, waiting for the Spirit to speak. Thomas told the kids, "Anything you hear the Holy Spirit say to you, speak it out loud." He explained to them that when they quiet their hearts before the Lord and ask God to speak to them, the Holy Spirit will whisper thoughts or give them pictures in their minds, and that they can learn to recognize His voice. The Spirit began to speak to Thomas and Marie through their kids. Sometimes they saw a picture, or God gave them a Scripture or a prophecy. Then the Spirit would give Thomas or Marie a revelation or an understanding of the prophecy. They learned to allow the Holy Spirit to lead them as a family.

Through all of this, Joy and Stephen learned to expect God to speak. The Scriptures began to come alive, not because they were reading them verse by verse, but because God was speaking through them. Joy and Stephen moved rapidly into prayer and prophecy and, on occasion, even into words of knowledge.

Things continued this way in their little church for a year and a half. Thomas thought that everything was wonderful—and it was—though he was leading it. As he let the kids interact more and more, he realized that Christ was taking over their times together.

One day, Thomas prayed a sincere but naïve prayer. "Lord, we're really growing as a family now, and I recognize there's more You want me to do. Lord, maybe we need to move on."

Then God spoke clearly to Thomas's heart and told him he hadn't really learned what it means to live a life in Christ. "You are being arrogant!" God seemed to say. "You need to listen more to Me and fall more deeply in love with your kids and your wife."

In retrospect, Thomas reflects, "You can sum it up like this. You can fall so deeply in love with the Father that it oozes out of you onto your kids and your wife. Timothy and Titus teach us that the elders of the church have that as the model of their lives. This is the criteria for leadership in the church, that a person understands how to give away his life to his wife and to his kids. This process took a year and a half to get through my thick skull!

"I really backed into all of this," Thomas continues. "It wasn't something I intentionally pursued because I'm smart. Leadership in the church in North America is based on position, privilege, power, degrees, or going to seminary. The Lord showed me that leadership actually is more like a father giving his life away to his family. As it is in the natural family, so it is in the spiritual family."

After three years, Joy and Stephen had memorized a lot of Scripture because of their desire for God; but more importantly, they knew how to hear God's voice. During that time, Thomas also discovered the BELLS model (Blessing, Eating, Listening, Learning, Signs and wonders). This model expresses one way of thinking about the main elements of a house church meeting. Each week, he blessed his wife and kids, they ate together, they listened to God and learned from

Him, experiencing the reality of knowing God's voice and seeing Him move. The phrase, "living in a prayerful expectation" began to speak to them about signs and wonders (where God works miracles in people's lives). They began to pray, believing God would move in these ways.

(Some readers may not be familiar with some of the terms used in this section. Things such as prophecy, revelation, words of knowledge are usually referred to as "gifts of the Spirit." They are detailed in 1 Corinthians 12. The ones described here are ways in which God may speak to people. For example, prophecy is a person speaking words that he hears God speaking into his heart or mind. The scriptural guidelines for prophecy are found in 1 Corinthians 14:3—prophecy is to be used for edification (building up), exhortation (encouragement) and comfort. The Scriptures instruct us to weigh prophecy; i.e., not merely to let it pass over our heads, but to assess whether it is from God and how to apply it to our lives. Words of knowledge occur when God supernaturally gives information about a person's life, and they are often used to cause faith to rise up in that person.)

A GROWING FAMILY

One day, about three years into this church life, a young couple came into Thomas's office, hurt and brokenhearted. They had just met with the pastor of the mega-church they attended to bring to his attention some indiscretions in the church. The pastor informed them in no uncertain terms that he didn't appreciate this—that it only made things worse. He asked them to leave the church!

"We are wondering if God wants us to be involved in a home church environment," they told Thomas. The couple, in their early 20s, had only been married for about 18 months. They were struggling in their marriage because of the controlling influence of the circumstances at the mega-church.

Thomas shared with them how his family experienced church. "We would like that. Can we visit you?" the young couple inquired.

"I think you need to go and visit some other folks. We're still pretty new at this. I know of three other groups closer to you who have been established longer," Thomas replied.

Three weeks later the couple was back in Thomas's office. "We still haven't found what you described and we really want it. Can we please come to your house?"

Then the Lord spoke clearly to Thomas. "Take them home!"

Thomas describes what happened next.

"That young couple came to be with us—and that was four years ago. It turned out to be the beginning of a new ministry for us that we had no idea God would call us into. They were really the prototype. It wasn't long before they brought another young couple with them, and Marie and I became their spiritual parents. We poured our lives into them and helped them with various issues. They were comfortable in our intimate setting. They referred to our home church as a "safe place"—a place where they could open their hearts and not fear people gossiping about them or having their hearts injured. We taught them how to bless one another, how to hear God's voice and understand what God is saying.

"I estimate we have had 50 to 60 couples come to our home in the past three years who have been touched by these ideas. Some stayed for a long time; others just visited for help or to observe a home church in action. Some planted other gatherings in different parts of the country. Now, in our local area, we have seven gatherings that have started from this first one, five to six of which are very healthy, and we're working on the others.

"Marie and I work with each one of the couples. We share with them that what people find so attractive is the way our family lives. They can live that way in their family, too.

"It's painfully difficult to be transparent with family and just as difficult to surrender your life to someone else. But when you do, you see the fruit and it becomes a great joy. When you see lives change, it's fantastic!

"As these couples begin to live this way, God attracts other couples to them, much like He did to Marie and me.

"Of the 60 or so couples who have been through our home, we have personally only invited three. We are not intentionally recruiting others to come. The Lord brings those He wants here."

Each week, those at the Sunday gathering at Thomas and Marie's home listen to the Lord and bless each other. Then during the week, Thomas (and sometimes Marie) spends time with people counseling them and doing "life discipleship." The focus is on each person's identity and destiny in Christ, and they explore such questions as: What does this mean for them as individuals within their family? What does this mean as part of the community of believers? How do they practice accountability and submit their lives to each other without legalism? Thomas goes through the principles in Luke 4:18 with them where Jesus says, "The Spirit of the Lord is upon Me because He has anointed me to preach the gospel to the poor; He has sent Me to heal the brokenhearted, to proclaim liberty to the captives and recovery of sight to the blind, to set at liberty those who are oppressed." Thomas and Marie believe that as these young people are set free, they will be able to set others free. Many of them will be carrying this DNA for the next 40 to 50 years.

SPIRITUAL LEADERSHIP

Thomas has a pastor's heart, a father's heart. He believes that he has to be a father first before he flows into the spiritual gifts. Thomas explains, "Otherwise, gifts become more important than heart. Without heart, the gifts get tainted. A simple and intimate life with the Father comes first, then life with each other. For us, the family is the first and most foundational expression of the church. God will then naturally wrap around a family other couples who need what they have. It is an expression of John 17. Then the "oikos" (your sphere of influence) community comes together, and this is the primary gathering of church."

He further explains, "When I first heard Wolfgang Simson describe leadership, the concept struck my heart like a ten-ton boulder! Wolfgang says, 'A true leader is like a weeping father, crying out for his sons to overtake him.' Servant leadership is a father pleading with God, begging on behalf of those in his spiritual family, crying out for his sons to become spiritually mature."

Thomas believes that from here, the churches he has helped start will become more missional, reaching out to the world around them. There is evidence this is already starting to happen. This is what he's longing to see. He is encouraging the people in the network to give away what they have. As this happens, his vision is to hand over the network to the "spiritual fathers" he has trained through life discipleship. He will be a "spiritual grandfather," keeping in touch with those churches and visiting them often, but free to start other networks elsewhere. He is also encouraging the people in his home church to start their own churches. "It's like kids going off to college," he says. "We're releasing them to start their own spiritual families."

Thomas is confident, that because these people know how to recognize God's voice, they won't merely follow a program. They will follow their Heavenly Father as He leads them step by step.

He says, "Our aim is to bring health to those we are consistently in fellowship with and to heal their broken hearts. Then they will see their destiny in the world. God speaks to them in most of our times together. They can hear Him say, 'I want you to go to that orphanage and help the kids there,' or 'Go under the bridge and help these people,' or 'Go to Starbucks and sit next to this guy and lead him to Me.' Ninety-nine percent of the Christians in North America cannot do that—after 20 years as a Christian, I couldn't do that! I had to learn how to hear God speak."

Thomas believes that those who become Christians in a simple church environment usually do so without religious baggage, but there is also a need for house churches that start with people from a Christian background. "We need both kinds of churches," Thomas explains. "There are 15 to 20 million Christians in this country who have given up on church. If they become healthy, they could lead house churches, and some of them would lead networks. We need to get them healthy and then release them to bring in as many others as possible!"

KEY THOUGHTS: CHURCH IS FAMILY

Church is pictured in a number of different ways in the New Testament. It is described as a body, or as a temple built of living stones. But probably the most commonly used metaphor is that of a family. (Ephesians 2:19) Paul often talks about himself as a father to the churches he has founded (I Corinthians 4:15), or refers to others as his brothers and sisters. (Romans 1:13)

In a family, life is informal. It is hard to picture a father at the meal table at the end of the day, talking for an hour without giving his kids time to interrupt. Church is life—family life. And like a family, it is relaxed and casual. Conversations ebb and flow. Family life adapts to circumstances.

Also like a family, simple churches are constantly developing. In a family, children are born. Older kids get married and move away. Simple church is the same way. Churches come and go. They give birth to daughters, or change according to circumstances, but the relationships remain.

Another principle to come out of Thomas and Marie's story concerns the nature of leadership. Thomas and Marie are a wonderful example of servant leadership. They live to bless and encourage others.

Jesus had some things to say about leadership. In Matthew 20:25, He describes how leadership works in the world. He says, "You know that in this world kings are tyrants, and officials lord it over the people beneath them." (New Living Translation) And we do know that is how it works in the world. In a business you have a C.E.O., maybe a C.O.O., then heads of various departments and finally the people who actually do the work. In the army you have generals, majors, captains and sergeants and finally, the rank and file corporals and privates.

Jesus goes on to say, "It shall not be this way among you!"

So what do we have in most churches? We have a senior pastor, associate pastors, Sunday school teachers, ushers and finally the lowly man in the pew. But Jesus said it was not to be this way! There is no clergy/laity distinction in the Bible. Instead there was a genuine priesthood of all believers. There were leaders; they were just of a very different nature than what we too often see today, and their purpose (at least those in traveling ministry) was to equip the people to "do the work of ministry." (Ephesians 4:12)

Jesus expands what He means by saying that anyone in leadership needs to be the servant of those he leads. He demonstrated this by washing His disciples' feet. (John 13:5) In these simpler forms of church, leadership is non-hierarchical. It is not based on education (except that gained in the school of experience), or on a charismatic personality or natural ability. Instead it is based on character issues such as how a person treats his family, or whether or not they are willing to open up their home for hospitality. (I Timothy 3:1-13) I also love how Wolfgang Simson describes leadership as a weeping father, longing for his sons to overtake him. Are we, like John the Baptist, willing to decrease so that He (and others) may increase? (John 3:29, 30) Are we willing to promote others above ourselves? Are we willing to lay down our lives for others? Are we willing to help others fulfill their vision rather than have them fulfill our own?

My observation is that God is training up a new breed of leaders. These are people who have spent time on the backside of the desert with God. They may have spent many years going through trial after trial, disappointment and disillusionment, not even able to hear God or understand what He is doing with them, yet loving Him with all their hearts. These are people who have died to themselves and to their own ambitions. They do not want the limelight. They fear to touch His glory. They are a people God can trust with leadership.

We need to cry out to God that this is the leadership that develops as this movement expands.

JOE'S STORY

The Kingdom at work

PROBLEMS AT WORK

"This is not the kind of professional behavior we expect from our employees! I hate to do this, but I don't have any choice. You are suspended from work pending further investigation."

The day started normally enough. Joe, a tall, well-built guy, worked for a long-distance telephone company as a team supervisor in their customer service department, responsible for a team of 25 people.

Andy, one of his team members, came to him just before lunch, obviously very upset.

"Joe, can I see you for a second out here?"

They stepped out of Joe's cubicle into the busy hallway where Joe could still keep an eye on his team.

"Joe, please pray for me. My uncle, the one who raised me, has had a severe stroke and he's dying. The doctors want to take him off his life support. I'm his only living relative, so I have to give my permission. I'm on my way to the hospital now. It's all up to me and I just can't bring myself to do it. If I say they can turn off the life support, he will die. What should I do?"

Tears were rolling down Andy's cheeks and his body shook with sobs. As they stood in the hallway, Joe put an arm around Andy's shoulder and prayed for him in a low voice.

"Lord, please help Andy know what he should do. Give him the courage to make the right decision."

Joe prayed with him quietly for two to three minutes, and then Andy left.

Two hours later, following the regular weekly team leaders'

meeting, Joe's supervisor came up to him.

"I heard you were praying on the floor earlier today. Is that true?"

Joe explained to his supervisor what had happened.

Before he even had time to get back to his desk, the boss of the entire center approached him.

"Joe, we have a real problem here. Someone overheard you praying with Andy and has complained. We cannot allow you to pray with people on the floor."

"Come on, this is ridiculous!" Joe exclaimed. "I was only trying to help one of my team members who was in trouble."

His boss explained that Joe was being suspended. "We need to hold a further investigation into this matter. But you will be suspended, with pay, until it is complete."

Joe was devastated. How was he going to explain things to his wife, Holly? She had coped with so much already.

Holly prayed for Joe for 11 years before he became a Christian two years earlier. At the time, Joe was working as a video store manager. Just before Christmas that year, Joe was at work during an ice storm. As he took out the trash, he slipped and fell on the sidewalk, breaking both his ankle and leg. He ended up in the hospital. He was released on Christmas day, but was laid up for weeks at home, unable to get around and eventually losing his job. With five children, this was a serious problem.

One Sunday morning in early spring, Holly said to him,

"The kids and I are going to church. Do you want to come?"

Holly had asked Joe to come to church with her many times, and Joe had always found an excuse in the past not to go. But by this time, he was so desperate to get out of the house that he would do anything, even if it meant going to church...So he accompanied them to the house church they attended.

The Lord spoke to Joe that morning. On that very first visit, without anyone preaching or praying with him, he surrendered his heart to Jesus.

The change in Joe's life was immediate. He stopped worrying! Before this encounter with the Lord, he used to stay up at night worrying about everything. Holly hated telling him if she was having car problems, for example, because she knew that sleepless nights would follow. But now, worry was a thing of the past.

Joe found the job with the long distance company shortly after this experience, and he progressed up the company ladder to a supervisor's job. He was known there as a Christian because he often had his Bible sitting on his desk. But now it appeared he had lost that job. Joe knew very few people had ever been reinstated after a suspension. So he and Holly could be facing more unemployment and the accompanying financial struggles.

But two weeks later, Joe was reinstated. They checked into his work to see if they could find any kind of impropriety. But his record was clean, and they could not fire him.

"We can't fire you for praying," they told him, "but don't let it happen again! If you come across another situation where you need to pray with someone or comfort them, you must find a private room and close the door."

"Well, are you saying that it's not a problem if I meet with people in a private room?" inquired Joe.

"Yes, that's what we are saying."

"Then how can I get a private room?" Joe asked them.

"You need to put your name on the list to reserve a room, and we will let you know if one comes available," was the reply.

So Joe put his name on the list to reserve a room, and thought little more about it.

CHURCH AT WORK

Joe's supervisor came to him a few months later.

"We have your room for you."

Sure enough, a room was reserved in Joe's name for lunchtime every Tuesday. Right away, he let people know that he would be holding a meeting for conversation and fellowship. (He did not use the word, "church" to describe it as this might have raised red flags for the management.) He wasn't allowed to put up flyers, but the word floated around that people would be getting together. And, of course, now Joe had a reputation for being a Christian! The company as a whole was studying one of John Maxwell's books as part of continuing management development, and Joe decided that he would use that book as his basis. Since the book is based on biblical principles, he would also reference the Bible. The company could not disapprove of them studying one of their own recommended books in greater depth.

A small group of people began to get together regularly. Then a second "church" started on a day when Joe was off. Joe sat in with them to help them get started. Then one of them was transferred to another city an hour away, and that person started a church in his new call center.

Then came 9/11.

That day, Joe was asked if he would lead the entire employee workforce in prayer before it shut down for the day. So Joe prayed aloud on the company's behalf for the victims of the Twin Towers and their families. When he went to the room for the regular lunchtime meeting, it was packed with people. There were around 30 of them jammed in there who wanted to pray for the nation. His boss was even there! Several of them became long-term members of the "church at work."

One day a few weeks later, traffic on the interstate came to a standstill while Joe was driving home from work. As Joe was sitting in his car listening to a CD, he glanced in his rear view mirror and saw a man get out of his car and approach the car behind him. Then he came up to Joe.

"Do you have a cell phone I can borrow?" he asked Joe.

"Sorry," Joe replied. "I don't carry a cell phone."

The man paused for a moment and listened.

"Oh, I love that song!" he commented. "It's Dennis Jernigan, isn't it? Are you a Christian?"

The two of them began chatting back and forth, and as Christians often do, he asked Joe where he went to church.

"I go to a church that meets in a home," said Joe, and explained a little about the concept. "But it's not limited just to home. I also have a small group that I meet with at the office where I work."

"Oh, can you do that?" the man asked.

Joe told him about how he started a group at his work.

"I could do that, too!" the man exclaimed. He was one of the owners of a business. He and Joe exchanged phone numbers.

A few days later, the man called Joe and asked if he would help him get a meeting going at his office. So for a few months, Joe helped him on his days off.

Joe's faithfulness resulted in four churches starting at work.

(After three months, Joe's company took back the room. So for several months, the group met outside around some picnic tables.)

Other amazing things have happened to Joe.

Karen, one of his team members at the long distance company, was known by everyone to be a Wiccan. People did not associate much with her, calling her "Witchy-Poo" behind her back. Karen started to ask Joe questions about Christianity. Knowing she didn't have friends, Joe sat and listened to her, hoping it might help her to know she was not alone.

"How can you believe without proof?" Karen would ask. "How do you know that it's God working in your life?"

Joe would turn the question around.

"How do you know it was the spell you cast that caused something to happen?"

Sometimes Joe told her that he was praying for her, but she would just respond by looking oddly at him.

One afternoon, Joe had a strong gut feeling that he needed to sit down beside her and talk. That particular day, she was crying and sobbing. It turned out she had boyfriend problems.

"I'm still praying for you, you know," Joe told her.

This time, she replied, "Thank you."

Joe had days off for the next three days. But when he next came to work, Karen was not there anymore. Nobody knew where she was. She just didn't show up for work.

Several weeks later, Joe was called to the reception area. When he arrived, there was a man he didn't recognize waiting to see him.

"I had to stop by and see you," he told him. "I am Karen's father. I want to thank you for giving me my little girl back!" And he told Joe this story.

Karen had decided that life was no longer worth living. She was pregnant, and considering an abortion. She had planned to commit suicide as soon as she got home from work on the day that she last talked to Joe. But when Joe had offered to pray for her, she changed her mind. Rather than going back to her apartment, she got in her car as soon as work was over and drove across the country to her home—with the suicide note still in her purse. Her parents were Christians, and after she arrived home, she re-dedicated her life to Jesus.

"So you see, you saved not just my daughter's life," Karen's father concluded, "but also the life of my unborn grandchild. When I found out I was coming to town, I just had to stop by and say thank you!"

GOD AT WORK

A considerable time after all this happened at Joe's work, the accident occurred. One cold, dark, winter morning, Joe was on his way to work early and stopped at a gas station to get some hot chocolate. Noticing that one of his tires needed air, he pulled up to the air compressor and got out of the car. Suddenly, a motorcycle sped through. To avoid being hit, Joe jumped backwards. But he tripped, falling and hitting his head on the concrete base of the air machine.

Joe was shaken, but went on to work. The only after-effect, apart from a splitting headache, seemed to be a nosebleed that would not stop. Later during the day, one of his managers saw him still dabbing his nose.

"Hasn't that nosebleed stopped yet?" she inquired. "You need to leave work right now and go to the Minor Emergency Center. We'll cover for you."

Joe may have had his first seizure in the parking lot of the Minor Emergency Center. The doctors performed a number of X-rays but couldn't find anything wrong. So they sent him home and told him to take a couple of days off.

Things escalated from that point, and Joe does not remember much of that time. He was no longer able to concentrate, could not multitask, and he started to have seizures—up to five or six per day. They were not typical seizures; he would merely go unconscious for a few seconds. Of course, he was unable to drive and had to give up work again.

Six months later, Joe was still in the same condition.

One night, he woke up to someone calling his name.

"Joe, Joe!"

Thinking it was one of the kids, he got up to check. They were all quiet, so he went back to bed and immediately fell asleep again. Then he heard someone call again,

"Joe!"

"Is that you, Lord?" Joe asked.

The Lord spoke to Joe and told him that he was being healed.

"You can throw away your pills, but keep the container as a reminder of what I have done for you," the Lord told him. He went on to inform him of various changes that would occur in his life, starting right away.

When he arose the next morning, Joe could not wipe the grin off his face. He was totally healed. He could concentrate again, and has never had another seizure.

One of the things the Lord told Joe is that he would run a store where people donate things he would either give away or sell. That is what Joe does now—he runs a consignment/thrift store.

A short while ago, Joe and Holly were at an auction buying things for their store. A rather ornate chair came up for sale.

"I am not moving on until someone gives me a dollar for this chair," said the auctioneer. So Joe and Holly bought a single chair for $1, and put it in the front of their store.

A week or so later, an older fellow they had not seen before came to their store. Joe greeted him and asked if he could help. He was doing some work out in front of the store when he glanced at the man and thought he must be having a heart attack. His face was very red, he was shaking all over, and he had to lean on the counter to steady himself. So Joe picked up the ornate chair.

"Here, you sit down. Are you OK? Do you need me to call an ambulance?" Joe asked him.

The man sat down and started crying as he told Joe this story. He had been married for 40 years, and his wife was dying. When they were first married, he had been with the army in Europe. He bought his new wife a table and a set of chairs while he was there, and had it shipped home for her. She loved it. One day, he was standing on one of the chairs to fix a light bulb and the chair broke. His wife was very upset, so he promised her he would find a replacement. And now, 20 years later as she lay dying, he was able to keep his promise to her. The ornate chair he was sitting on was identical to the set he had bought for his wife.

"You can have it for three dollars," Joe told him.

But the man insisted on giving him a $20 bill and would not accept any change.

This kind of thing happens frequently in Joe and Holly's store. You see, God is interested in what happens at work, too.

KEY THOUGHTS: THE KINGDOM AT WORK

In the Lord's Prayer, we pray, "Your Kingdom come, Your will be done, on earth as it is in heaven." We are praying that the Kingdom of God would be worked out here on earth, in every part of life. But then we divide our lives into sacred (what happens when we are at church or when we are spending time with the Lord) and secular (what goes on all the rest of the time). For Christians in New Testament times, there was no such separation.

Joe's story illustrates that from God's viewpoint, there is no difference between sacred and secular. God is as interested in what goes on at work (or during our recreation times) as He is in what happens when we get together as His church. If we will let Him rule in every area of our lives, He is able to bring His Kingdom authority to bear where our lives intersect with the world.

Back in England, Tony frequently saw this happen when he was a practicing doctor. He would often pray with his patients and many of them—probably literally hundreds over the years—found the Lord in his office. During one six-week period, a patient became a Christian every day!

At one point, all the family doctors in the country received a letter from the General Medical Council (the British medical licensing body) stating they were changing the rules concerning patient confidentiality. Up until that time, if a girl who was a minor wanted contraceptives or an abortion, the doctor was obligated to obtain parental consent (just as he would if she needed surgery for an ingrown toenail). But the letter said the girl's wishes for privacy in these areas now had to be respected, and the parents were not to be informed without the minor's consent.

Tony called a few other doctors who were in leadership within CiCP, the organization that he ran, and they all agreed this was not acceptable. So Tony wrote a letter to the GMC explaining that he represented about 2,000 family physicians, and that they were not prepared to see centuries of accepted medical practice (to say nothing of the Hippocratic Oath) overturned in this fashion. He wanted them to know up front that he and the doctors he represented would not obey this edict; and, if necessary, the GMC could remove their licenses to practice medicine.

A few weeks later, he received a conciliatory letter back from the GMC saying they had no idea that some physicians felt so strongly about these issues, and that of course they were free to follow their conscience without fear of reprisal. The kingdom of medicine was being brought under the authority of the Kingdom of God!

What might have happened if all the Christian teachers in America had refused to buckle under the ruling that prevented prayer in schools?

God wants "the kingdoms of this world to become the kingdoms of our God and of His Christ." (Revelation 11:15) If we are willing to live for the Lord at work, we will be amazed at what He can do.

Joe continues to see the Lord use him in his place of work to demonstrate the Kingdom of God. He is living out his Christianity in relevant ways in the marketplace.

STUDENT
STORIES

Service and strategy

JORDAN'S STORY

Jordan took a deep breath as he knocked on the door of a fellow student's dorm room—his first one! He and a few friends were trying an experiment in their residence hall at the University of Texas. As the door opened, a blast of music hit him. A somewhat disheveled youth wearing jeans and a T-shirt proclaiming him to be a freshman peered out.

"Hey, my name is Jordan and I live down the hall. Can I take out your trash?"

There was shocked silence for a few seconds.

"Why are you doing this?"

"We're a group of Christians living down the hall. We follow Jesus, and we think He would probably take out people's trash. We want to serve the people on our hall and get to know them."

"Well, I guess so. I hate taking out my trash. Cool!"

As Jordan emptied the overflowing trash cans into the large black sack he was carrying, he reflected on what had led up to this point.

The previous semester, he and another friend, also a sophomore, decided to live in one of the dorms on campus. They wanted to be very intentional about ministry and reach out to the people they lived around. They came up with several ideas for how to contact them. One in particular caught their imagination. They heard about someone at another university who picked up people's trash once a week as a way to initiate a relationship with them. He then invited them to a Bible study. The students respected him for serving them practically, and the group grew as people began to follow Christ.

Jordan and his friend decided to try this out. They shared with

171

a couple of Christian girls down the hall their vision of building a Christian community to serve the people around them. About 100 people lived on their floor and they settled on a Thursday night to go door to door and offer to take out people's trash. Now he was actually doing it!

"There's a group of us going bowling on campus later tonight," Jordan added as he was leaving the room. "Would you like to join us?"

Fifteen people—contacts from the evening's trash collection—went bowling together that night. Jordan knew a couple of them but most were strangers.

That started "authentic faith community." Each week, the Christians collect people's trash in the dorm and look for others to hang out with. Each week they invite people to play board games, eat together or get involved with other activities when they finish collecting trash. Several people who don't know Jesus also collect trash with them now, and 15 or so regularly hang out with them.

Half way through the semester, Jordan put up a poster on his door inviting people to a Bible study on the parables and teachings of Jesus. Seven or eight of the people they have contacted through trash collection and who are more spiritually hungry come to that. There is no formal teaching; they just read a parable and talk about what it means and how it can affect their lives. This has led to some genuine discussions on the meaning and purpose of life, and a couple of girls are close to following the Lord. They now read the Bible on their own, and join in the prayer times at 7:00 one morning a week.

CAMPUS STRATEGY

Campus Renewal Ministries (CRM) is a group that seeks to network different ministries on the University of Texas campus. It is not a campus ministry in itself. About 45 ministries work at UT, and CRM helps them stay in relationship with one another and seek God for a common strategy to reach the campus. Justin, who works full time with the ministry, describes a little of its history at the university.

"In the year 2000, a group came in to spiritually map the campus to identify the distinct subcultures on campus. We also surveyed each of the ministries working on campus to see what was happening collectively and which groups the different Christian ministries were reaching. We decided that every October we would ask someone in to advise us and interact with us to help us come up with new vision steps for the coming year.

"In the fall of 2001, various campus ministers realized their ministries needed to shift from what we termed a "come-to" church to more of a "go-to" church. We started thinking about how that might look and how we could help the different ministries on campus move in that direction. At that time we wrote a vision statement for a campus saturation plan that read, "We want to see a viable Christian community in every college, club, residence and culture at our university." That has continued to be the vision statement behind what we do. It hasn't been easy. The first year we did very little, but in the last two years we have made some headway.

"Last year we did a survey and found there are 500 different communities on campus. The agency that worked with us on this project came up with eight different cultural profiles of the students—from "creatives" (artistic types) and "gym rats" (athletes who associate with the physical activities in which they engage), to intellectuals. We are in the process of developing and refining a "family tree" for each of these groups. For each group—the "creatives" for example—we find out which colleges within the university tend to have that profile of student, where they live and where they spend their time. We treat the whole family tree as a foreign mission field. We attempt to have Christians intentionally live where those groups live or hang out where they congregate in an attempt to minister to them. The Christian students deliberately go to places where there is no witness yet. They try to form "authentic faith communities," a term all the different ministries working on campus are happy to use for groups that form.

"Most of the Christian students involved in the authentic faith communities, especially the leaders, are also committed to different churches. But for fringe people, this is their church. We use the expression "authentic faith community" rather than "church" because we are trying to use a term that everyone can accept. All the different ministries working on campus use that term and all of the AFCs are networked together.

"This is a long-term plan. The end goal is for every student in the university to have a relevant Christian community to interact with during their four years of college. Of the estimated 500 communities we are trying to reach, 60 of them have AFCs (in essence, simple churches). Only 440 more to go!"

HUAN'S STORY

Huan is another student the Lord is using to start an AFC. He lives in one of the smallest dorms on campus. Three years ago, another Christian student who was working in the dorm as a Resident Assistant with 30 students assigned to him, invited some of the students to go to church with him. He loved them and took time with them, and eventually started a small group that came together to study God. Many of the students wanted to do great things in their lives, and he invited them to come and seek God about this.

The next year, Huan took over the Resident Assistant position, and he took students to this same small group. Huan is from mainland China, and he works a lot with other Chinese students. Many of them are facing difficulties in transitioning to life in the U.S., and they come to him broken and in despair. Huan shares with them how hard it was for him, how God has transformed his life and has the power to change their situations. He demonstrates his love for them by hanging out with them, and sharing his life with them. Every day they eat or work out together, and on the weekend they do different activities together. As Huan shares with them what God is doing in his life, he finds these students also want to get to know God. Several have become Christians.

Huan is in the petroleum engineering department, and he is also working with others there.

A group of Muslim students from Indonesia are very suspicious of Christians. But Huan shares every aspect of his life with them, including what God is doing with him and the difficulties and challenges he faces. Because they have been working on projects with him for two years, they have seen how God has changed him. Huan loves them and respects them. He knows he cannot change them, but he faithfully prays that God will work in their lives. Many of them talk to him or go home with him. Huan is very sensitive to them and invites them to hang out with his Christian friends.

"You are different from a lot of the Christians I've met," one of them told him. "You respect me and love me, but other guys make fun of me."

"How are you able to stay joyful when you go through challenges?" they ask him.

"It's because God makes so much difference in my life," is his reply.

Several of them are about to graduate and return to their home country. Huan is praying that before they go, they will want to know this God they have seen making such a difference in his life.

Every Thursday night, his AFC meets to study the Word, share their lives together and pray for one another. They also serve their community by collecting trash and sweeping floors.

Huan loves to disciple his fellow students even before they become Christians. As he hangs out with them, playing video games and sharing meals or working out with them on a regular basis, he finds it usually isn't long before they respond to the genuine love they sense from him. He then invites them to a more purposeful study on how they can go deeper with God; soon they give their hearts to Jesus.

Run by the students and without rules, the university co-ops tend to be a little wilder; there is a lot of drug use and sexual activity. Three years ago, an AFC started in one of the co-ops. As the group met together and prayed once a week, they left their door open and people started coming by to hang out. Many unbelievers came by to worship and to pray and be prayed for. Again, some became followers of Jesus.

Last year the Christian group started doing something powerfully radical. The co-op has a reputation for its wild parties. When the party is over, the place is totally trashed. The AFC decided they would be the ones to serve at the parties and clean up at the end. So they greet people at the door, serve the drinks, do all the things needed to keep the party running and then clean up afterwards.

This has had profound spiritual significance. People still talk about it today. And the students in the co-op know the Christians pray on a weekly basis for their neighbors. They know where they can go for prayer or help.

CRM trains those leading the AFCs once a month. The training is designed to help people live more intentionally and missionally with the group in which they hang out. Not all of the groups are full-fledged AFCs yet. Some are like a pioneer mission with one or two students trying to build relationships, although there is not yet enough spiritual interest to start a seeker group. But many are catching the vision, and the AFCs are continuing to expand.

JAESON'S STORY

Other groups around the country are seeing similar moves of the Holy Spirit.

Back in 1998, Jaeson, a freshman and a new Christian, was sitting in his Philosophy 101 class of several hundred students.

"Who here believes that Jesus Christ is the Son of God?" the professor asked.

Jaeson immediately raised his hand. But as he looked around the room, he realized that he and one other friend were the only ones to do so. Jaeson was shocked, and he began to pray for hours every day, prayer-walking the campus and crying out to God for the more than 28,000 students there.

God soon began to open doors for him, and the student government actually sponsored him to hold evangelistic events on campus. Hundreds of students were touched and gave their lives to Christ. But few of them subsequently became part of a healthy local church. Jaeson pondered the problem for a long time.

In his research across different campuses, he found a common problem. Most of the students thought church was "boring, irrelevant and hypocritical." Yet at the same time, many of them were hurting and broken. In their desperation for meaning and reality, many turned to partying, drugs or sex in an attempt to fill the emptiness and find some purpose in living.

After graduation, Jaeson worked for a while at a tech job, but soon quit in order to focus on missions work. This changed his perspective on church, as he began to see some very different models of how people gather. He realized that the simple, relationship-based churches he saw in countries such as China or India, where people shared their lives together on a daily basis, would be intensely relevant in a student context.

"If an 18-year-old, uneducated, Chinese girl can plant 100 churches a year, why can't a college freshman plant a few churches on his campus?" he thought.

Jaeson started a ministry called Campus Church Networks (CCN). The purpose of CCN is to train students to start campus churches that reach out to those around them in the U.S. and different parts of the world. If a student can be trained to win his network of friends to Christ and start a small church, and that student can then train others to do the same, this could multiply and spread like wildfire. It could reach into every segment of the student population and transform campuses.

This is already beginning to catch on. Michele, a campus church planter who works with CCN and YWAM in Colorado Springs, is seeing God ignite spontaneous prayer groups that focus on praying for repentance and revival.

It all started when a morning prayer group, in conjunction with a similar group in another college, agreed to confess 2 Chronicles 7:14 over the campus and the nation at 7:14 every morning. (This verse says, "If My people, who are called by My name, will humble themselves and pray, and seek My face and turn from their wicked ways, then I will hear from heaven, and will forgive their sin, and heal their land.) Groups of students get together at 7:14 a.m. to pray this prayer on various campuses around the nation, and it is spreading. They have a vision of 714 groups all over the country seeking God in this way, and hope to implement a 24/7 prayer model on the campus. They know campus churches will be planted as a result.

The students of today are the leaders of tomorrow. If we can reach them while they are in college, they are the ones who will change their communities, cities, and eventually the nations. Many moves of God have started with students. Could He be doing the same thing again?

KEY THOUGHTS: SERVICE AND STRATEGY

This story demonstrates two interesting principles. The value of service is the first of these. Many simple churches are starting as people find unique ways to serve their communities. Mission Arlington, near Dallas, Texas, is a network of more than 250 churches—mostly meeting in apartments, mobile homes and neighborhoods. Those churches exist because 18 years ago, Tillie Burgin decided to serve the poor in her community and provide for them in practical ways. Tillie helped a lady with her utility bill and some other practical needs, and that led Tillie to teach John 3:16 to the lady and 16 of her friends. A church was born from that group.

Service costs us in time and convenience. What price for spreading the Kingdom?

The importance of an intentional strategy is the other principle this story illustrates. CRM will know when it has accomplished its objectives at U.T. They will know when each of the groups they are trying to touch is reached. They have a plan and they are going for it in many different universities across the nation.

As simple churches, we are often afraid of strategy because we confuse it with programs or denominationalism. We think that if we will just follow the Holy Spirit, we will accomplish His purposes. When Jesus sent out the 70 to all the different places He was going to visit, do you think He had a plan? Obviously we need to seek the Lord for His vision and His plans for our area. And we need to be dependent on Him, with every move bathed in prayer and open to change. But there is great strength in having a vision and strategy for what He wants us to do.

The International Mission Board of the Southern Baptist Convention is seeing multiple church planting movements emerge in many different nations, at least in part because they are willing to strategize under God for that nation. We have much to learn from them.

More information on the organizations mentioned in this story can be found at the following websites:

Campus Renewal Ministries   www.campusrenewal.org

Campus Church Networks   www.campuschurch.net

KRISTIN'S STORY

Stone soup church

EVERYONE IS IMPORTANT

Kristin was sitting at her desk, going through the emails on her computer.

"Hey Dear, listen to this!" she called out to her husband, Phil, who was fixing dinner in the kitchen. "It's from that home church mailing list I belong to. They're going to start a house church over here on the west side."

Phil strolled over to the computer, and Kristin read the email aloud to him.

"Greetings,

We are inviting all those who would like to meet with other people who are interested in forming an expression of God's church on the west side of the river. Some of you may have visited or attended meetings, but have had to travel east to do so. Some of you are curious and have not visited a house church before. This is for everyone. We are not experts, by any means. Just lay people following a direction we believe God has been calling us to.

"We ask that each one come with their thoughts, impressions, songs, giftings... and we will see what God has to say to us. We are all members, each with a part. Staying with this theme, my husband and I thought we would have a "stone soup" meal. For any of you who have never participated in this type of meal, you're in for a treat. Here's how it works. We begin with a pot of water and a large (clean) stone. Each one brings their favorite vegetable, spice, etc. to add to the soup. The finished product is a unique combination of "favorites." Note: No backyard mushrooms, or surprise veggies that may or may not be edible!!! Tea and coffee will be provided. Perhaps someone could bring some French bread.

Andrew and Alison"

"I've wanted to try something like this for a long time, and we're between churches. Let's give it a try," suggested Kristin.

Kristin had been a churchgoer for many years. But church had become empty and non-relational to her, and something she attended out of duty because she was supposed to. A couple of times she and Phil dragged their feet so long on a Sunday morning they arrived at church in time for the closing prayer!

A few years ago, she read a book called *The Open Church* by James Rutz. Since that time, she has sensed that a group of friends meeting together over a meal and talking about Jesus is probably closer to what the New Testament describes when it uses words such as "ecclesia" or church. She was not excited about the idea of eating together or sharing about Jesus with friends, but she longed to actually say something, to be empowered to contribute, to discuss the Bible and its challenges. She wanted to be real about her own life, her neighbor's life, and not just discuss the Sunday sermon.

So the following Sunday afternoon, Kristin and Phil were parking their car and knocking on the door of an immaculate-looking home a few minutes away. They received a loving welcome from hosts Andrew and Alison, and were made to feel right at home. They were not the only ones who had responded to the email. There were seven of them that first night, all total strangers to each other. Each person brought something to put into the soup and there was much laughter as they added their contribution to the stone sitting in a pan of boiling water. After half an hour or so, the soup was pronounced ready to eat.

They sat around the big dining-room table, enjoyed the steaming bowls of soup and crusty bread and learned a little about each other's lives. All of them had been Christians for some time, but for whatever reason had either given up on traditional church or were between churches.

That first afternoon, they talked about church and what it really means to be a church.

"Church is different from a Bible study," commented one person.

"We should do more than just look at the Bible. It includes prayer and fellowship, too. And we need to be free to share any problems we might have so others can pray for us."

"It's not some kind of a group therapy session, though," said another. "And I think everyone should be able to contribute."

"Yes, everyone was important in the New Testament church," someone else added. "It says that everybody has a part to play and that we all have something different to bring."

"It's kind of like the soup we made tonight, isn't it?" said Andrew. "Just like with the soup, we are starting from scratch. God has brought a group of people together and He can make us into a caring community. Not only that, but whenever we get together, everyone brings a contribution, and the Holy Spirit takes what each person supplies and makes it into a meal to nourish us spiritually."

So they decided to continue meeting as a "stone soup" church. They did not stay strangers for long; the Holy Spirit developed them into a community that loved and cared for each other. Week by week, each one brought something towards the meal. And week by week, as each one of them brought their spiritual contributions, the Holy Spirit spoke through one and then another. Each person learned to recognize His whisper in their hearts, and each one knew that when the Spirit spoke, they were responsible to bring to the group what He was showing them. It might be a thought from the Bible, or a song; it might be a picture (a visual representation of a concept the Lord was trying to communicate) or a prayer request. As time went on, they learned to overcome their shyness, and experienced the Holy Spirit orchestrating their times together.

Sometimes, however, their meetings were not so exuberant. Everyone might be tired. They would crawl in from their weeks and expect God to show up. Occasionally someone was so tired, they would actually fall asleep!

God was usually present, however, and being led by the Holy Spirit was never boring. In fact, it spoiled them all for any other style of meeting; only a round-table format satisfies now.

Kristin felt for the first time in her life that she could say and really mean, "I was glad when they said to me 'Let us go to the House of the Lord.'"

(Right from the start, Andrew and Allison let everyone know that eventually they were called to go on the mission field. When that time came, about 18 months after the group's commencement, the "stone soup" church blessed them and sent them out. At that point, people chose not to continue as a group but go wherever the Holy Spirit led each person.)

KEY THOUGHTS: STONE SOUP CHURCH

In our network of simple churches, we base our gatherings together on Acts 2:42 where the disciples "continued steadfastly in the apostles' doctrine and fellowship, in the breaking of bread, and in prayers." So our gatherings together include a meal, fellowship, time around the Word and prayer.

Chapters 11 through 14 of I Corinthians discuss how the church should function together. These chapters are well worth studying in greater detail, but I am just going to highlight a few points here.

In 1 Corinthians 12, Paul uses the metaphor of a body to describe the church (verses 12-27). He states that, just as a body has many members and each one is significant, so it is with the body of Christ, the church. Each person in the group is important, and each has a different contribution to make. We are not looking for conformity, but diversity, the different gifts of each person acting synergistically together to produce a whole. No one would want a body consisting only of eyes or ears. Everyone is important.

The functioning body of Christ is like an orchestra, with the Holy Spirit acting as the conductor. The richness of a symphony occurs because all of the different instruments in the orchestra play the melody assigned to them. If we all play the same tune in church, we miss out on the magnificent creativity of the Bride of Christ.

But Paul goes beyond that. He says that the weaker members are necessary and worthy of greater honor. The contributions of those who are shyer or more reticent to speak should be given greater attention.

Of course, the head of this body is Christ, and as each person follows the prompting of the Holy Spirit, the body functions as it should. You see, the Lord wants to be given more than lip service in our meetings. He actually wants to be in control.

If we are not careful, house or simple church gatherings can run like a traditional church meeting. Someone has been asked to lead the worship, another has been asked to teach...The venue has just changed from pews to couches. But that excludes a major dynamic of a small group meeting; i.e., that the Lord has a plan for our times together. He knows what is going on in people's lives. If we will let Him, He will touch and change people and the world around us. A time together, led by the Holy Spirit, is never boring.

God has given us the pattern for this in I Corinthians 14:26, which says that each person should take part and bring a contribution to our time together. (This is one of the reasons that we are so sold on the concept of church being small. That would be impossible in a larger gathering.) I Corinthians 12 and Romans 12 are packed with the idea that every member is important to the functioning of the body.

But how do we follow the Holy Spirit in a meeting?

Let's say that we are sitting in a meeting, and someone has just prayed a great prayer full of praise to God. What should happen next? How can we know what the Holy Spirit wants? In our experience, the best way is to make that person's prayer our own vehicle of praise to God. As we do that, if a verse of Scripture or a song comes to mind, chances are the Holy Spirit is speaking. On the other hand, if we are thinking, "Well, we haven't sung a song in a while. There must be a good one that would fit with that prayer," that is not as likely to be Him. In other words, if we fully participate in what is going on, the things that come spontaneously to mind are most likely from the Holy Spirit. We should expect variety—gifts of the Spirit such as prophecy and visions, prayer for each other, insights from the Scriptures, etc.

God is very creative! And don't be concerned about making mistakes. Nobody will mind if we do, so let's step out and try something new!

In most legacy churches, people are trying to raise the bar. So whether it is the worship, the teaching or the qualifications for leadership, they are aiming at a higher standard of "excellence" or quality. Sadly, this means that fewer and fewer people can participate. We are trying to lower the bar so that no one is prevented from taking part because they feel they could never perform well enough.

The simpler something is, the easier it is to duplicate. If Andrew and Allison had produced a gourmet meal that first week, it would have sent a message. "If you want to start a church, you have to produce a spectacular meal." Instead, the message was "Open your home and everyone will bring something."

The same applies to other areas, too. If you have a skilled guitarist who leads the worship, the implication is that you can only multiply the church if you have a good musician. If one person does all the teaching up in front of everyone, then you can only start a daughter church if you have a good teacher.

This is why, in nearly all of our churches, we rarely have someone stand up front and give a talk. Instead, we study the Scriptures together interactively (for example, using the question mark, candlestick and arrow described in Lisa's story). The symbols aren't that important, but they get everyone talking. And when people share what they see in the Scriptures, they are learning. You see, in legacy churches we get hung up on having good teaching. That is missing the point. The vital thing is that people learn. Studies show that people learn best when they participate. Not only that, but as the person facilitating the study constantly points people back to the Scriptures rather than answering questions himself, people learn that the Bible—not the person teaching—is the authority.

If a Christian joins one of our churches, it is quite common for them to comment after a few months, "I have learned more in the past three months than I learned in three years in a traditional church!"

In simple churches we are trying to lower the bar of how we "do" church so that more and more people can participate. Simple is not the same as shallow. Some of my most profound spiritual experiences have come in a simple church context. When the Holy Spirit is free to work as He wills in a gathering of disciples, the effects can be profound. On the other hand, simple can be duplicated. If a few easy-to-follow patterns are established early-on, then almost anyone can facilitate a time together.

I love what a Filipino church planter says: "I never do anything in church that a one-week old Christian would be unable to do!" Think of how that applies to our praying, (no more five-minute-sermon prayers) or to our sharing what the Lord is doing in our lives (no more Christianese).

We multiply what we model. Let's keep things simple and multiply rapidly.

NEIL'S STORY

Discipleship and training

NO HOME

"You'll be back here!"

Neil was sitting in a meeting in Long Beach, California when the Lord clearly spoke these words into his heart. Not only did the Lord speak plainly, but he gave Neil an impression of the house he and his family would be living in; in fact, Neil knew the exact residence!

Neil grew up on the beach. He had been a lifeguard for several years, and he loved the ocean. He actually lived in Long Beach once for ten years. But he had moved away and become a pastor in a conventional church. Two years earlier, the Lord put on his heart that he would be returning to Long Beach.

Because of Neil's strong leanings towards discipleship and church planting and mission, he had been training someone with more of a pastoral heart to take over his position as pastor of the church. That way, he would be free to plant churches. He had a vision to multiply small groups in an organic fashion—organic churches. He wanted to work in an urban area with a large university population because he wanted to reach young people; and he was looking for a city with a beach (for baptisms, of course!) Long Beach fit perfectly.

Neil had a team of a dozen people going with him, and a set of well-laid plans as to what they would do. He and the team were going to start a coffee house they would use for evangelism. In fact, they already had the location.

Not only that, the house Neil sensed he was supposed to be living in became available! So he and his wife packed up their house, and set out with their three kids, Lacey the dog, a cat, a bird and all their possessions. They were ready to go into the coffee house business!

But there was a problem when they went to pick up the key to their new house.

"The current tenant has decided to remain in the property," the owner told them.

Now what were they going to do?

Neil and his family were homeless! They stored all their possessions in the coffee house. The family slept on borrowed couches when they could; they went to a cabin in the mountains for a couple of days, and for two weeks they stayed in a motel room.

While they were living in the motel, Neil was responsible for walking Lacey twice a day. Each night, he used to stroll to the top of a hill in the middle of the city. He was surrounded there by the sounds of the city—gun shots, cars screeching, people yelling at each other, dogs barking, sirens. The sounds reverberated into his heart, and he found himself weeping for the city and for the shame and darkness there.

"Lord of the harvest, send workers to this city and change this place. Carve a church out of the darkness," he would beg God, his heart breaking for the city.

"I did not send you here to start coffee houses, but churches. Find an existing coffee house and pray a church into being there," the Lord told him. So much for their business plans!

After seven weeks, the tenant eventually vacated the house. When the family was finally able to move in, someone even picked up their motel bill for them. Neil now reflects about that time,

"It was God's way of teaching us that we had to follow His way rather than pursuing our own plans."

Their new home did not have a yard, and Neil still had to exercise Lacey. On one of these walks he found a coffee house about four blocks away. He and the other team members started hanging out there daily, drinking coffee, playing games and listening to people's stories. And they prayed.

The team members met for church in Neil's home. At 12 adults, it was already too large and was still without a convert. But their mission to reach the city was clear. The emphasis was heavily on evangelism. Every day, team members spent time at the coffee house getting to know its clientele.

The first night that a non-Christian—one of their coffee house contacts—came to the church, she observed what went on:

"I go to a large church all the time, but God is here in this place!" she remarked.

The next week she brought her best friend, who brought her best friend, who brought her best friend—a chain reaction! And one by one people began to come to Christ.

Brad was already a Christian when he came for the first time. He was hungry to do church in a different way, and wanted to reach the city, make disciples and multiply groups. He had never before seen a church that could do that. He visited once, and never went back to his old church. One meeting changed him forever. One year later, he started a network of organic churches.

MANY HOMES

In just a short time, Neil's living room was filled with both new and older Christians, so they commissioned a group to start a church in a second coffee house called Porfirio's.

Porfirio's turned out to be the hangout of a witches' coven and various satanic groups, such as vampires (some drink blood, file their teeth down or sleep in coffins!). Two churches started from this new place. The second of these was in Michael's home. (This became their healthiest church, because they had learned from the previous two what not to do.)

Many people had been praying for Michael, including his wife. As a younger man, he had once prayed a "prayer of salvation," but had never really experienced the Life of walking with Jesus. Michael had a painting business, but he also had a drug habit that consumed him and caused him to lose everything. His truck was repossessed, his house was foreclosed, his business went into bankruptcy and all his employees left. His wife was fed up with people either doing drugs or obtaining drugs at their house and stealing from them. Finally, she had had enough. Wanting to practice tough love, she also left him and went back to her mother in Mexico. Michael was at rock bottom.

One day at Porfirio's, one of the team members bumped into Michael and told him about Jesus. The message got through, and Michael fell on his knees and gave his life back to Christ.

On the beach in the freezing cold that December, Michael baptized four new converts who used to do drugs with him. Neil believes the church was born at this point.

Neil intentionally separated the group meeting at Michael's house from all the other Christians. He wanted it to be a church born out of the harvest, namely out of Michael's relationships. The church was very evangelistic and grew quickly. It was kind of messy; it had no music and no gifted people. Neil was the only mature Christian involved. All of the others were either new believers or pre-Christians. He tried encouraging a new Christian to lead the worship there, but he quit. So they started without music, and with only the friends Michael reached.

Another church started out of the one at Michael's house in a low-income apartment complex. But as people became Christians, they moved out because they didn't want to stay in the ghetto; so it lasted only about a year.

But in the past six years, the church in Michael's home has started 20 daughter churches, several grand-daughter churches and a few great grand-daughter churches. They have trained missionaries and sent them around the U.S. and to other countries—such as France, North Africa, Kosovo, Spain and Jordan. One of their daughter churches sent a missionary to Thailand.

Why are these churches multiplying so rapidly?

"The lines of churches with this kind of reproduction are very harvest-oriented," Neil observes. "They start with non-Christians, and the people who come to the Lord are trained right from the start to reach out to their circle of influence or 'oikos,' the Greek word in the New Testament often translated as "household."

"The other major factor is our use of Life Transformation Groups (LTGs). We find these make a big difference."

LIFE TRANSFORMATION GROUPS

Neil developed LTGs when he was in a conventional church. Knowing that disciple making was the key to church growth, he experimented with different ways of making disciples. He used every curriculum he could find. But he would get bored after the third or fourth time through it. He didn't want the people he was discipling to be bored, so he developed his own curriculum—and got bored with that even faster! He spent a lot of time creating it, but he was already fed up with it by the time he used it. It sits on a shelf in his office now as a testimony to the futility of that year!

Neil then brought together a group of people once a week to discuss whatever Christian book was new and interesting. He was soon tired of that, too. Although that might add to people's knowledge, it was obvious it wasn't going to change anyone's life. That was not enough!

"What book could anyone read that would transform their life?" he asked himself one day.

At that moment the light went on. "They're going to read the Bible!"

He told his group to put their other books away

"I want you to read the whole of the book of Proverbs before we get together again," he said to the group of three college students at a coffee house.

"That much in one week? Don't you know it's 31 chapters?" they questioned.

"Yes, the whole book in one week," Neil insisted.

Part of Neil's reasoning for using the book of Proverbs was that one of the young men he was working with was an extremely angry person. None of the other books they had been using addressed that need in his life. The book of Proverbs talks a lot about foolishness and anger.

By the next week, Neil had read the whole book. It blew him away how powerful it was to read the entire book in one week. As he read, he designed symbols to put by the verses to make it more user-friendly. If the verse was on money, for example, he put a dollar symbol beside the verse. If it was on communication, he drew a tongue, or if it talked about anger or violence, he drew a pair of angry eyes. The book of Proverbs came alive to him.

The students, however, read only six or seven chapters.

"You need to try this; it's powerful!" Neil told them. "Let's start again at chapter one and read it all the way through this week. Try using these symbols."

Neil read the entire book again the next week. He gained even more insights, and the book was even more alive. He couldn't wait to share with his students again. This time, no one had read even 10 chapters.

"Okay, we're going to keep reading Proverbs until all of us finish it in the same week," he announced to them in frustration.

Then it dawned on him: "That's not a bad idea!"

In four weeks, they had all read the entire book of Proverbs in one week. At that point, Neil had read it all the way through four weeks in a row. It was changing him.

"I found wisdom pouring out of my life in every kind of situation," he says.

But he recognized that the one student still had an anger issue. The book of James addresses anger.

"Let's read James seven times in one week. That's once a day," he instructed the group.

After reading the book of James 48 times, the angry student left the group. But there was another kid, Kent, who had a drinking problem. At the age of 20, Kent already had a D.U.I on his record. He had been involved in an accident and his license had been revoked. His life was circling the drain. Kent gave his life back to Christ. He immediately took to the Word and began to grow.

Neil met with Kent and another kid who had come out of Mormonism for a whole year. When the other kid left and went to college, Neil encouraged him to continue reading on his own. He did for a while, but then Neil stopped hearing from him.

Meanwhile, Kent was really growing. Then came the week they were supposed to read through Romans twice in one week.

"Did you read Romans through twice," Neil asked Kent at their regular weekly meeting.

"No, I didn't finish it," he said. But he had a smile on his face.

"How far did you get?"

"I read it all through once, and the second time through I read fifteen and a half chapters."

"But Kent, why didn't you finish the last chapter? Romans is only 16 chapters long!"

"Because I want to read it again!"

What a change! This is a kid who is now hungry for the Word. It isn't enough for him to read through Romans twice in a week. He really is beginning to grow and change.

Around this same time, Neil was also studying the life of John Wesley and the history of Methodism. He was interested in how their groups multiplied, and particularly about what they called their "class meetings." (This was John Wesley's early system of lay-led small groups.) He liked how the class meetings empowered ordinary people to lead groups. The leaders did not have to be pastors. There was a list of questions that anyone could ask, and everyone in the group answered. Neil didn't think the questions would work in a modern-day context. But intrigued by the idea, he adapted a list of questions he found in a book and added some more.

"When we used the questions to confess our sins to one another," Neil explains, "we started to see spontaneous multiplication.

"I was trying to grow the group into a large Bible study of maybe 10 or 12 kids, but it wouldn't happen. Every time it grew to five or six, it would shrink back down to three people. Always to three. But then we found we were multiplying without even trying."

One day, Neil went alone to the restaurant where the group usually met. He sat down at a table and pulled out his Bible to spend some time with the Lord.

"You should be really proud of Kent. He's doing great with his group," Mary the waitress said to him. (She would later become a Christian.)

"Kent has a group?" questioned Neil.

"Yes, every Monday morning he meets with a bunch of people here. I remember Kent before you all started meeting together, and now Kent 'after' is quite a change!"

Neil was astounded. It kept echoing through his mind, "Kent has a group? Kent has a group!"

Neil contacted Kent.

"What's this I hear about you having a group?"

"I just started doing with some of my other friends what you do with me," he explained.

Kent's group grew into a larger group that broke down into several smaller groups. Those groups then continued while Kent started another group in a different place with different people. They copied the list of questions, and soon several groups met and did the same thing.

Bible reading and the accountability questions formed the basis of the Life Transformation Groups. Prayer was the last thing to be added.

Neil had developed a leadership training program that took a person step-by-step from conversion to being a church planter. It was not a curriculum in itself, but a set of self-study materials for a leader that could work in any context. It helped him assess what tools he needed to make disciples, leaders, leaders of leaders, church planters, missionaries and pastors. LTGs were introduced as part of the training program. But as it went to press, the Lord put on Neil's mind that there was a missing piece—prayer for unbelievers. So after a quick trial run, prayer for unbelievers was added. An LTG now consists of reading large portions of Scripture, accountability questions and prayer for unbelievers.

The LTGs started to spread. Very few people bought the leadership system. But within one year of its publication, LTGs were starting all over the world. People took the tape that mentioned LTGs, copied and distributed it.

One of the kids who came to Jesus at Porfirio's was a young man who had been involved with drugs. He started two churches. He had an aunt and uncle who were pastors, and one day he went to visit them. They were very excited he had turned his life around and gave him a tape to listen to. It had been used so many times that the label explaining who was speaking on the tape wasn't legible.

The young man started the tape.

"I think that's my pastor," he told his aunt and uncle. Then he listened further.

"Yes it is! It's Neil!"

LTGs are one of the main reasons that Michael's church grew so rapidly. They used them from the very beginning, and it was the foundation for changed lives. Neil determined the church would grow because of transformed lives and not by staged events to attract non-Christians. They used LTGs from the moment someone came to Christ (and sometimes even before they were Christians). From the start, the new Christians were reading large quantities of Scripture (or listening to an audio version, if literacy was a problem), praying for their friends and confessing their sins to one another.

Every church that has grown out of the original one at Michael's house has started this way. Confession of sins results in new life, and reading the Scriptures further transforms people. Even after six years, everyone in the church at Michael's house is still in LTGs and they continue talking about what they are learning from them.

Most people who use them have given up on them for a period of time. But a few months later they realize, "I need what LTGs do in my life; I'm going to start them again!"

MENTORING AND TRAINING

Leadership and training are the other concepts that Neil has spent considerable time thinking through. In the traditional church he was part of, he created a leadership development system for training leaders within the context of the local church. But after it was published, the Lord spoke to him about it.

"I want you to do it again from scratch, but with new converts this time."

So when Neil moved, he was not interested in starting churches as much as he wanted to create leadership farm systems.

"I wanted to produce leaders that would start organic churches that develop into movements," he explains. "That involves mentoring and coaching church planters out in the field, and creating resources to help them while they are on the job. That's how 'Greenhouse' started. My co-worker, Paul, worked with me from the beginning to develop leadership farm systems for those starting organic churches. What has emerged is two weekends of training along with local monthly meetings. We have related everything to the principles used in gardening and farming—hence the 'Greenhouse.' We even use the term 'organic church' rather than house church, which has too many negative connotations in this country. People tend to associate that term with a small, inward-looking group of disgruntled Christians rather than a vibrant and missional church.

"Mentoring is very important in raising leaders for the harvest. Organic mentoring is dictated by the needs of the person being mentored, rather than a program designed by the mentor.

"I find that early on, a new Christian is eager to be mentored, but he hasn't done anything yet. I don't spend a lot of time with him at this stage, but I throw out the challenge for him to do something in ministry. I'll spend time with him informally at church; then when he becomes fruitful, I will take more time with him.

"If I find someone very excited about serving the Lord, I'll say to him, 'Go and win someone to Jesus and start an LTG with him.' When they have done it once, I tell them to do it again. They can multiply these groups and start a church. At this point, when they have followers, I will mentor them. The mentoring process at this stage occurs once a week or every other week. As they grow more and more fruitful, they become more time conscious, and they mentor others. Then I shift to mentoring them once a month, and coaching them quarterly. Finally I will say to them, 'Just call me if you need something or if a crisis arises.' Or maybe I will bump into them at a conference and spend time with them. It's a layer-upon-layer progression as they begin to invest in others and become less and less needy and dependent on me.

"It's a very organic process based on the needs of the person being mentored. When we first developed it in a traditional church context, we called it 'the pastor factory' and it was very inorganic. I realized early-on that a cookie-cutter approach cannot work because people are different. But we had no way of knowing that before we got out there and got our hands in the soil and found out through practice. Unfortunately, many books on the subject are written by people who haven't done it. It's all theory, and it doesn't work.

"Many years ago we tried to start a church using conventional church growth methods. We produced a full-color brochure that went to thousands of homes in a new community. We had a worship band and did everything right. But it failed, and we realized we had not been planting a church, but trying to buy a church.

"When the LTGs started, we realized we were planting seed. It was a much more organic approach to raising leaders for the harvest. Mentoring waters that seed so it can bear much fruit.

"Greenhouse teaches that the best soil in which to plant seeds is where people are most needy. 'Bad people make good soil—there's a lot of fertilizer in their lives!' So we need to be out in the fields, where the soil is good, planting seed. The seed of the Kingdom is the Word of God. We are looking for a 'person of peace,' someone who will open up their circle of influence to us and who will be the laborer within that people group."

Greenhouse itself is producing an abundant harvest. Neil can track more than 500 churches that have been planted by people who have gone through the training over the past five years.

KEY THOUGHTS: DISCIPLESHIP AND TRAINING

If churches are going to multiply rapidly, they need to be simple. Simple is reproducible; the more complex something is, the harder it is to duplicate. LTGs produce outstanding results in people's lives. But more than that, anyone can start one! Their genius lies in their simplicity.

Discipleship and training are important. Jesus spent much of his life with only 12 men. He lived with them, ate with them and shared His heart with them. They saw Him cope with every kind of person and situation. Much of the discipling process consisted in answering their questions. He gave them tasks to do and instructions on how they were to be done.

New Christians do not need mere head knowledge. They do not need our Christianity 101 courses. John 17:3 says, "This is eternal life, that they know You the only true God, and Jesus Christ whom You have sent." As the new believer spends time with us in the presence of the Father, he will learn to know Jesus and how to recognize His voice. As he studies the Word with us, he will catch our hunger and love for the Word. As he watches us heal the sick, he will gain faith to go and do the same.

The second part of Luke 11:23 says, "He who does not gather with me, scatters." A friend of ours in India tells of some interesting research. When a major evangelistic crusade comes to an Indian village, many hundreds of people may become Christians. However, if you follow up a year later, the churches haven't grown. Instead, the Indian temples, which may not have had much activity prior to the crusade, have all increased and become livelier. It's as though people have become more spiritual, but because they have not been gathered into communities, the end effect has been to scatter them.

An important part of the follow-up of new believers is that they are gathered into small communities where they can grow. It may be as simple as two or three sharing their lives together in some kind of accountability group where they read (or listen to) Scripture, share their struggles and pray for their friends. This provides a safe place from which the new believer can be encouraged to reach out to his old friends. New wine needs new wineskins.

Further information on Life Transformation Groups and Greenhouse training can be found at www.cmaresources.org

JIM & CATHY'S STORY

Kingdom finances and Kingdom kids

NO MONEY TO HELP

Jim and Cathy started a church in their home because of finances! Twelve years ago, Jim was an elder in a successful church of 1,000 members. He and his wife, Cathy, and their kids never missed a service; they were faithful to be there every Sunday morning and evening and also on Wednesday nights.

People were filing out of the beautiful sanctuary one Sunday morning after the service. Jim and Cathy were approached by Doug and Ellen, a middle-aged couple and good friends who had also been involved in the church for a number of years.

"Hi Doug, hi Ellen, how are you doing?"

"I was hoping to see you," Doug said. "I need to talk with you. Do you have a minute?"

"Sure," replied Jim, noticing that they looked a bit anxious. "What's on your mind?"

"Well, it's like this. As you know, I got laid off from work three months ago, and I haven't had a paycheck since September. We've run through all our savings and the credit card is maxed out. And Christmas is coming up! I can't pay the bills, let alone have any-thing to go towards Christmas. I was wondering if maybe the church could help tide us over. It would only take a few hundred. What do you think?"

"Have you filled in the church paperwork requesting consider-ation for benevolence?" asked Jim.

"Yes, I filled it in a couple of weeks ago, but I haven't heard anything yet."

"I'll look into it for you."

Jim knew that Doug and Ellen were not the only ones in this predicament over the Christmas season. But he was a little skeptical about whether or not the church could help. Because of his involvement on the church's leadership team, Jim knew a major focus of the church was the management of its money. The leadership meetings were more about raising money than they were about ministry, and all of the money seemed to go to the new building and the salaries of the full-time staff.

There was a leadership meeting scheduled for the next evening, so Jim was able to bring the subject up with the senior pastor and the other elders. As they sat in the pastor's comfortable office, he approached them with Doug and Ellen's story.

"I'm sorry, Jim, but we just don't have any spare money available to give to this kind of need," the pastor said.

"But our budget is over one million dollars! And these people have been faithful members for many years. I'm confident they have tithed regularly. Surely there's some cash somewhere that could be made available for them," Jim protested.

"We do not have any funds to help them!" the pastor insisted.

Jim was not happy! Surely this couldn't be right. Wasn't the church supposed to be helping its members who were in trouble? He ended up assisting Doug and Ellen through another small group of which he was a part.

"What is the church?" he asked the Lord. "I don't want to participate in a church that can't help its members. Please show me what a church is supposed to be."

Jim is a successful businessman, and the economics of the church didn't make sense to him. So he re-read the New Testament, especially the book of Acts, to see what happened with finances in the New Testament church.

A few evenings later, when their six children were in bed or happily occupied, he and Cathy were relaxing over a cup of coffee in their living room. Jim adjusted his glasses, put his feet up on the coffee table and brought up the subject again.

"In the New Testament church, no one had a need," he told Cathy. "It tells us in Acts that if anyone had anything extra, they brought it to the apostles' feet, and it was distributed to those who had needs."

Cathy looked at him, intrigued by the concept.

"So all the money didn't go on buildings and salaries," she commented.

"I've been seeing things in the Apostle Paul's ministry, too. It says in First Thessalonians that Paul did not take offerings from the Thessalonians, but worked day and night so that he could be a model or an example for them," said Jim. "He wasn't a financial burden to them at all. Paul was bi-vocational; he worked as a tentmaker. In Asia, he not only paid his own way, but also that of his team."

"There must be some kind of ministry that models what Paul was talking about," Cathy added.

"Yes, I think so. For the first time I've started to see in the Scriptures things like, 'Greet the church in so and so's house.'"

"So the early church used to meet in peoples' homes. But there are no churches that meet in homes these days."

"I don't begrudge our time at the church. Being faithful members there has built in us a strong walk with the Lord. But if we really feel this way, I don't see how we can continue going there," concluded Jim.

"Maybe we could start meeting in our home and see what happens."

HELPING THEIR CITY

The more Jim looked into things, the more unsettled he felt about their church situation. It took only a few weeks for him to resign from the board of elders at the church. And then he and Cathy felt the Lord nudging them to do something totally different.

Jim and Cathy started meeting in their living room with their six kids. Initially, they didn't approach home church as the New Testament model, or even as a better way to minister to people, but as a financial model that made more sense economically. It did not take long before others joined them. At a certain point in time, they started to collect offerings. Then they incorporated as "The Association of House Churches," with the understanding that anyone joining or leading a house church was committed to being bi-vocational and working in a secular job, as well as serving the church. A part-time secretary who handles the administration a few hours each week is the only person they ever paid a salary.

"We also came up with a mission statement based on economics," says Jim. "It says 'We will become a 1,000-member church, meeting in 50 to 80 homes with 80% of our money going to benevolence and missions, both local and foreign.' We are not yet a 1,000-member church, but we have kept true to the financial part. Over 80% of the money that is given goes to helping people and missions.

"We support eight local missions in our city and we are involved heavily in India. We give to missions in Haiti, and we help some of our people that go on short-term mission trips. And of course, there is benevolence. We feel we have a church where no one is in need, because if anyone does have a need or an emergency crops up, we have money set aside to help them as part of our budget. We're able to help those not only in our own fellowship, but others they may know who have financial needs. Right from the start, the Lord highlighted an economic emphasis in what we do.

"At one point, we made financial commitments to different ministries of a certain dollar amount per month. But then we found ourselves in a similar situation as many churches. If our giving was down for any reason in one month, then we were stretched to meet our commitments. So six or seven years ago, we went to a model where we break our giving into percentages. Whatever comes in each month goes out. For example, instead of giving $250 per month to one ministry, we'll give 5% of what comes in to that ministry. It has enabled us to increase our giving to different ministries because the percentages have grown as the fellowship has grown. And the ministries pray for us because as the Lord blesses us, we in turn pass it on."

The Association has had a positive effect on their city. They are the only church to give to certain secular ministries that help people in their city. For example, only two groups give on a monthly basis and volunteer at a mission that feeds one hot meal a day to the homeless—one is the Association of Home Churches, and the other is Dan's Biker Bar, a night club for bikers. Other people give occasionally, and the mission does have fund raisers to support the work. But working alongside Dan's Biker Bar has enabled the home churches to interface with people who never will wind up in traditional model churches.

"When we first started, no one knew what a house church was," explains Jim. "There was a lot of suspicion, especially among the churches. Their leaders would ask, 'Who is your ordained pastor and to whom are you accountable?' But our giving has brought us real credibility in our community. The Mayor knows about us, and we are received in a lot of places because we take our funds and help different social works in the city. We support the Crisis Pregnancy Center, the Mission Soup Kitchen, a homeless center that takes people in off the street, and a local drug and alcohol center that helps to turn around people who are caught in addiction. Some of them are Christian-based and others are secular-based ministries.

"Our support for church planters in India has supported more than 350 church starts. The ministry we have worked with there for many years uses more of a traditional model. But we are now partnering with someone who is working towards a more rapid, house church planting model. We often send people there, but they pay their own way."

Finances are not the only area in which Jim and Cathy have been pioneers.

Cathy is involved with the Crisis Pregnancy Centers. She is now the executive director of four pregnancy centers, two of them in their city, which is home to the largest military installation in the nation. These pregnancy centers may be the busiest in the entire country because of the large military population. The home churches play a vital role in this as members volunteer and make monthly financial contributions to the ministry.

Cathy sees her work there as an outreach to the mothers. Many of the girls (around 50%) have a Christian upbringing, but have become pregnant. At their initial session, the counselors discover whether the girls are involved in a church (most are not), and try to find out how they can help. From there, the girls participate in parenting classes. After the baby is born, they can get involved in mentoring groups that teach them life skills and help them to connect.

They used to send the girls to local churches. But they quickly found that little or no follow up was done, or the girls would never make it to the churches. So now, although they don't call it church, they have meetings at the centers where they bring together the girls to study the Bible. This has been life changing for some of them. Working on this with a number of area churches also provides an opportunity to partner with other Christians.

KIDS OF THE KINGDOM

When Jim and Cathy meet people who are new to house church, they tell them two things: "More people meet in homes than in buildings worldwide" is the first thing they say to them. And the second is, "One of the things we value most is the effect of this model on our kids." They have six kids, and all of them but the oldest have been raised in this model of church. All of them either are, or have been, in leadership at one time or another.

"They are not spectators but part of the church. They *are* the church! It's not just our own kids; others growing up in this model recognize they are the church. They don't just come to watch, but are actively involved in every level of ministry.

"During our times together, we purposefully go out of our way to have the kids participate as much as possible. They have the same Holy Spirit, and they are as much a part of the meeting as the adults. If they can read, we'll have them read some Scriptures; or they may pray with someone, or choose a song.

"We may separate the younger ones to go out with someone if people are talking. But as soon as they are old enough to comprehend, they participate. Once they are old enough to read, they can participate.

"Some visitors came recently, and we all gathered around one individual to pray with him. The visitors were astonished at the level of maturity in prayer of a bunch of eight- to 12-year-old kids. They were praying in the Spirit and interceding dynamically over this individual. We see that kind of maturity at a young age because we purposefully direct our focus to the kids. They know they are as important as the adults. Not just the adults hear from God—they do, too!

"A prophetic word given by a kid has even pushed a meeting in a particular direction. We just ask the kids, 'What do you feel the Lord is saying?' They can talk just like anyone else and whatever they say is valued. Kids are very sensitive to the Holy Spirit. Our youngest daughter, now 18, is a senior in high school. Because of being a part of this for the last 12 years, she has already led a number of people to the Lord and she is becoming quite prophetic.

"We have seen people who haven't stayed with this model of church because a bigger church has more activities for their kids. They have youth programs and Sunday Schools. The family may come for a few meetings and not really participate, and then they go back to the traditional church.

"But the number one benefit for this Dad and Mom has been to see what has happened to our kids. They haven't been to youth groups, although we do join with other ministries and larger groups so they can participate in bigger events. And we may have special meetings for kids. As they have grown into their teen years and gone on to college and beyond, they aren't content to be mere spectators. Because our kids have never been shuffled off into another area as unimportant, they have been energized from an early age. And now, they are leaders in whatever situation they are in."

KEY THOUGHTS: KINGDOM FINANCES
AND KINGDOM KIDS

Whenever we tell someone we are involved in a network of churches that meet in homes or anywhere that people live their lives, it's usually not long before they ask one of three questions.

"What do you do with the kids?"

"What happens with finances?"

"How do you prevent heresy?"

Jim and Cathy's network of churches is a great example for an answer to those questions.

We love the fact that simple churches, without buildings to maintain or salaries to pay, do not have to focus on acquiring funds in order to survive financially. Instead, they are able to give the majority of their finances directly into missions or benevolence. Usually the only time we mention finances in any of our gatherings is if we become aware of a need. Last week for example, we were asked by a church in the projects if we could help with some bills someone had following a car wreck. This was a family member, not someone who has come to that church or become a Christian. We took up an offering right then. When two of us took the church check (made out to the garage) to the lady concerned, we prayed with her and her family. She broke down in tears and has asked us to come back and pray with her on a regular basis. (Could this be the start of another church?)

Training kids spiritually is primarily the parent's responsibility. It isn't something to be delegated to a Sunday School. Obviously, it helps to be part of a community of believers. The main principle with kids is to include them in everything possible. As Jim and Cathy say, "They do not have a junior Holy Spirit; they are the church."

In our times together, usually it is the kids who will choose the songs. If we are going to pray for someone, they will join in laying hands on that person and praying for them. However, if we are studying the Bible, it might be more appropriate for them to do something else—play quietly in the same room, play outside, watch a video, or maybe do an activity prepared by an adult in advance. Each church needs to hear from the Lord on these issues.

As to the third question, "How do you prevent a church from moving into heresy?" we answer with a question of our own.

"Where do most heresies begin?" As people think about it, they realize that most heresies that have gained a grip on a church have occurred when a major charismatic leader starts promoting an idea. A small group meeting in a home is not likely to pose a threat. And if Scripture is the authority within that group, rather than the leader of the group, our experience is that heresies are very unlikely. The rest of the group will soon make the necessary corrections.

ALLEN'S STORY

To transition or not to transition?

THE BUSINESS CLUB

Two years ago, Allen went to an investment seminar where a speaker was teaching on how to strategize for tax savings. He was interested in what the man was sharing, so he went up to him when the seminar was over.

"How can I get you to work for me?" he asked.

"I charge $200 per hour, or you can join my business club!" he replied.

So Allen joined the business club which met in a nearby city, thinking he would have the opportunity to rub shoulders with other people involved in investing. They met every Monday night. They had a meal together, and one of the members shared on a topic of interest. The member's input often had a New Age emphasis. After a break, they moved to the subject of finances and investing.

"What am I doing here?" Allen wondered. One evening, he went home and prayed about it.

"These people are searching for God! Hey, there could be an opportunity here," he realized. So he began praying that God would open a door for him.

At one of the meetings, a lady stood up and began talking about the Buddhist teaching of feng shui, how the positioning of objects in an office can produce blessing in a business.

"What am I going to say? How can I counteract this?" Allen thought to himself urgently. After noticing some remarks she made about how certain buildings feel dark and heavy, he went up to her at the break.

"Your comment about buildings feeling dark and heavy is really interesting. I've also experienced that, but my way of dealing with it is probably a little different," he said.

"What do you do?" she asked.

"I pray over the place in the name of Jesus and command the evil forces to leave," he replied.

The lady looked shocked and obviously didn't know how to respond. She turned away to talk to someone else. But as she did, a smartly dressed lady in her early 50s came up to Allen.

"I couldn't help overhearing what you were saying," she said. "My name is Linda, and I'm in real estate. I have this house that I just haven't been able to sell. I'm sure there's something dark in it. Would you come and clear it out for me?"

"Well, OK. I could do that."

The next day, Allen met Linda at an older house that was empty except for a table and four chairs in the dining room. Linda was carrying a bag of candles.

"Oh no, she thinks we're going to have a ceremony here," thought Allen.

"Wow Linda, the candles won't be necessary," he said. "I'm just going to pray over every room in the name of Jesus."

So Allen prayed in every room. He commanded the darkness to leave and invited in the presence of Lord. As he went from room to room, Linda was very quiet.

"Does she think I'm nuts?" Allen wondered. He finished praying though the main floor and the basement, and was on his way upstairs when the front door bell rang. Linda went downstairs to see who it was, while Allen finished praying through the rooms upstairs.

When he went back down, one of Linda's clients was with her. He was looking for a house to buy.

As Linda introduced him, she told the man, "Al here is clearing out my house. Doesn't it feel better already?"

They chatted for a few minutes and then Allen asked, "Linda, can I pray for you, too?"

He sat her down in a chair, laid his hands gently on her shoulder and started to pray softly. As he did, the Holy Spirit came and Linda started to shake and cry.

"Something is happening here," he thought, and he began to pray the darkness out of her life. When he was done, Linda quieted down and said, "I haven't felt so light in years! Can we go for coffee?"

In the meantime, her client had been sitting in the corner watching all of this with a bewildered expression on his face. The three of them—Allen, Linda, and her client (who turned out to be Jewish)—headed for a coffee shop. For two hours, Allen answered the questions of a Jewish man and a New Age lady. He explained to them about the Kingdom of God, salvation and forgiveness.

The next week at the club meeting, Linda spotted him across the room, and ran over with a big smile on her face.

"Al, you have to get on the speaking roster at the club. You have to tell them everything you told me last week."

Allen wasn't sure what to do. But he went over to Susan, one of the organizers of the meetings. Just as Susan was about to turn toward him, Allen saw a lady walk through the back door with a cane.

"Susan, what's wrong with Jane? "Why is she walking with a cane?" he asked.

"She has a problem with her leg that won't heal."

"You need to let me do some teaching on healing."

"We could do that," Susan replied.

The following week, Allen sent Susan an email explaining what he would like to do.

"I will share some stories of healings that I have seen, including my wife's back. I'll share how I was introduced to healing and the paradigm I'm coming from. Then I'll do a clinic and pray for people."

Allen was surprised when he received a telephone call from Susan later that week. She explained that the speaker due in two weeks had cancelled, and asked if he would like to fill that slot.

When the evening came, Allen was terrified.

As usual, the group meeting started with a meal, and then one of the organizers introduced Allen.

"As you know, in this club we believe in having an open mind. I don't necessarily agree with religious things, but we have a man of the cloth here with us tonight," said the emcee.

Allen stood up. The people looked bored, as though they were expecting to waste half an hour.

As Allen started sharing stories of healing, everyone in the place was riveted. For half an hour he shared tales of God healing people, which gave him a chance to share the gospel. While he was sharing about the gospel, a man from the Middle East jumped to his feet and interrupted him.

"I used to be a holy man, too!" he exclaimed. He reached into his briefcase and handed out pictures of himself as a holy man. Finally he sat down and Allen continued.

As his time drew to a close, Allen said, "You know folks, I have just a few minutes left and this is going to take a risk on your part and on my part. I was praying this morning and God showed me five conditions here in this room that He's going to touch. I want you to take a risk and come up here, and I'm going to pray for you."

Allen then shared five conditions, including migraine headaches, chest pain and knee problems. Five people came up to him.

Allen took a deep breath and said to them, "This isn't up to me; it's up to the Holy Spirit. We're just going to invite Him to come, and we'll see what happens."

He invited the Holy Spirit to come as he prayed with people, and He showed up! Allen saw the evidence in front of him. Some of the people started shaking; others became teary eyed. The audience sat there with their mouths wide open.

Then he interviewed the people for whom he was praying.

"What are you experiencing?" he asked them.

"I feel hot all over," said one. "I can feel energy going up and down my leg," said another.

After the meeting, people made a beeline for Allen. One lady asked him for prayer. Another man asked if he would meet later to pray for him.

The following week at the club meeting, people came to him again to thank him and tell him how impressed they were. During the introductions for that week's speaker, a man came in a bit late and interrupted the proceedings.

"I'm still trying to process last week's presentation," he stated. "There are only three options. Number one, it was the power of positive thinking; number two, this was a serious case of mind control;

or number three, we actually had an encounter with the God of the Bible. If you're planning on doing any more talks like this, count me in."

At the break, Allen stood up and asked if he could have a minute.

"A number of you have expressed interest in what happened last week. We run a course called Alpha. It talks about relationship with God and healing. If anyone is interested, let me know."

At that point, Linda jumped to her feet.

"I'll host it!" she said.

At the first meeting at Linda's home, five people showed up. The group took several weeks going through the Alpha Course, which is designed to help people discover the basics of Christianity in a non-threatening environment. Several of them have given their lives to Jesus. As a result of the group, one couple even destroyed thousands of dollars worth of occult paraphernalia and books. The group continues to meet.

SHALL WE TRANSITION THE WHOLE CHURCH?

Two years prior to this, Allen was pastoring a church in one of the newer denominations. One day, he received notice from the landlord of the church property that he was increasing the rent—doubling what it had been!

"There has to be a way to start churches that doesn't take so much money," he sighed to Kathie.

Around that time, the church hosted a speaker for a weekend conference on healing. His final message was that people should go out to preach the Kingdom and heal the sick. While the speaker was reading the relevant Bible passage, Allen was struck, not by the part about healing, but by Jesus' words, "Go! I am sending you out!"

"We are not supposed to have healing meetings and invite people to come. We're supposed to take this to them in some way," he realized.

He went home with this idea in his heart. When he arrived back at his house, his brother was there. Also a pastor, Allen's brother was in the process of starting a cell church in his city, and had already started a couple of groups.

"How long do you think before you have a Sunday celebration?" Allen asked him.

"I'm having so much fun having church at the house, I don't know if I want to have a celebration," his brother replied.

"That's it, Frank!" Allen exclaimed. "If we start churches in houses we can do it everywhere and it won't cost us anything in real estate."

The next day he asked his secretary to go onto the Internet and find out everything she could about house churches. The research revealed some interesting results.

Allen determined there were two flavors of house churches out there. The first seemed to proclaim, "We have found the New Testament church and we're doing it right. The rest of the existing church is doing it wrong, and we want to let people know that." The second kind expressed things more along the lines of, "We think we've found something here that could work to advance the Kingdom." Allen was more interested in the latter, and started researching and reading anything he could get. As he studied, he became more and more convinced this was the way he wanted to go.

At first, Allen thought about transitioning the whole church. However, a house church leader he respects gave him some different advice.

"Why in the world would you want to do that? Most people in your church didn't sign up for that. If you lead people down that path, it's going to kill you and it's going to kill the church. If you want to plant house churches, then *you* go do it!"

Allen approached the leadership team at his church and asked if they would release him to start house churches.

"I feel like I'm a church planter at heart," he told them. "I loved my first four or five years here. But now I'm just in maintenance mode, and it's killing me! I just have to do this thing. Will you release me to go and do it?"

A team of leaders assumed leadership of the church. Allen also felt that if he was going to ask ordinary people to start and lead house churches while they supported themselves with a job, he needed to model that himself. He asked the church if they would cut his salary to one third and he went back into construction.

Two other couples from the church wanted to join in the adventure, and all of them were sent out by the church as a church planting team. For the first couple of months, they met together to pray and seek God. Because they were mostly families, they assumed they would grow by reaching other families. But when they started an Alpha course, young, single people attended. Allen's secretary, a single mom, had caught his heart for the lost by working with him. She invited her daughter, who brought some friends. They ran a second course, and the group now consists of the original three couples, plus the new converts from the Alpha courses.

Allen retains his good relationship with the church he pastored. The two house churches—the one started by the team, and the other that grew out of the business meeting—are counted as an outreach from the church. Allen still preaches at the church every couple of months, and what is happening there as a consequence is interesting to note. For years, while he was pastoring there, Allen preached to them about the need for outreach. People often looked at him with a blank stare. But now when he tells them stories about what God is doing, it stirs them up. They, too, have started Alpha Groups in some of the surrounding towns, and numbers of people are coming to the Lord. But the new believers are staying in their local groups rather than coming to the central church. The people who lead the groups remain a part of the central church, but that church is content for those won through this outreach to stay in their home churches.

Not only has Allen had an impact on his local church, but his denominational leaders at a national level have given their blessing. They are open to exploring alternative ways of planting churches, and have invited him onto a national task force on church planting so he can influence what is going on.

Could God have plans to change a denomination?

KEY THOUGHTS: TO TRANSITION OR NOT
TO TRANSITION?

What happens when the leader of a legacy church catches a vision for a simpler model of church? Should he transition the whole church? What about his position? Is he now irrelevant? Usually his family's livelihood depends on the church. Unlike Allen, he may not have the training or skills to change jobs. Or what happens if a legacy church has members who sense God is telling them to start simple churches?

Jesus gave an interesting illustration. Luke 5:37-39 says this. "No one puts new wine into old wineskins; or else the new wine will burst the wineskins and be spilled, and the wineskins will be ruined. But new wine must be put into new wineskins, and both are preserved. And no one, having drunk old wine, immediately desires new; for he says, 'The old is better.'"

There are several interesting points in this parable. First, Jesus showed an equal concern for the new and the old wine— and consequently, the new and the old wineskins. Jesus is as concerned about our legacy churches and the people who attend them as He is about simple churches.

Jesus says that new wine needs to go into new wineskins. When people become Christians, they usually will do far better if they can remain in a small, simple church that is relevant to their culture, unless they have become a Christian within the four walls of a legacy church. If we expect them to get involved in our traditional churches, we not only stand a high chance of losing them, we are failing to seize an opportunity to reach into their sphere of influence and sub-culture.

So, should we try to transition the whole church to the newer model? According to Jesus, if we do that, we may ruin the old wineskin and spill all the wine.

It is significant that Jesus said if people are used to the old wine, they always will prefer it over the new. Church history shows the truth of that statement. Very few churches are able to sustain a lasting transition to any new theology or practice of church. Hence, denominations! In the early days of the charismatic movement in the UK, a number of churches tried to change their services to reflect what God was doing. A few made it, but the majority quickly reverted back to their old ways. The people didn't want to change, and their pastors were not willing to risk losing them. Most of the Christians determined to change started or joined new churches. Now, 30 years later, it is not an issue. Nearly all evangelical churches are very open to things of the Spirit.

So what does a leader of a legacy church do when he catches a vision for multiplying simpler churches?

He and the church need to seek God for answers, and obviously God can tell them to transition the whole church. There are a few models currently of those who have done it successfully. However, any church could do what Allen has done. The church can free people from the pew to start simple churches as an outreach from their legacy church. But the release needs to be complete and unconditional, no strings attached. If the church insists that the person remain fully involved in the parent church and bring in his new people, the leadership will hinder what God is doing.

I believe God will bless a church that gives away their best people to mission. He is debtor to no one. He will quickly replace both the people who leave (and their finances)! And the Kingdom of God will advance.

LES'S
STORY

"No empire building, no control and no glory"

MULTIPLICATION

"Les, could we get together some time? You know we're moving to a new house next month to be nearer my daughter?
Well, she's asked me to help her start a church in her home, and I am
wondering if you have any ideas about how I could go about it."

"Sure, Jim! How about lunch together tomorrow?"

As Les hung up the phone, he reflected on yet another opportunity to help someone start a simple church. He had known Jim
for a number of years now. Jim was fairly typical of the fastest-
growing segment of Christians in this country—those who do not
go to church. He loved Jesus with all his heart, but was floundering
somewhat since leaving the traditional church. This could give some
real direction to his walk with the Lord, Les thought.

The restaurant was crowded, but Jim and Les found a corner table where they could talk undisturbed. Once the waitress had taken
their order, they got down to business. Les flattened his napkin on
the table and pulled out a pen.

First he drew two parallel lines of small boxes on his napkin.

"These represent the homes along a street." He put an "X" on
one of the "homes." "Just imagine that you lead someone in this
house—we'll call him Bob—to the Lord. If you then introduce Bob
to the church you attend, he has to go down the road, across the
railroad tracks and way over to the other side of town."

Les drew an arrow from one of the houses toward the edge of the
napkin.

"Bob gets so busy in your church that he has no time left for the
people on his street. Now imagine, instead of taking him across

town, you start a church in his home. And one of the aims of that church is to reach his neighbors and family."

Les drew some arrows from Bob's house to some of the other houses in the street.

"Then you have reached that community for the Lord," Jim said excitedly.

"Now, suppose Bob's friend from work becomes a Christian. Should you bring him to Bob's home?"

"You could, but it would be more effective to start another church in his home!"

"You've got it! That way, you reach another community of people."

"Things could multiply very quickly if that really caught on!" The light was obviously going on for Jim.

"Now let's go back to Bob's house," said Les. "Let's imagine that the church in Bob's house starts to grow, and it gets so big that it no longer fits in Bob's living room. What would you do?"

"We could divide it into two," Jim suggested.

"That would be one possibility," Les agreed. "But there might be a better way."

He turned the napkin over and drew a circle.

"Let's say this represents Bob's church. This is what you are suggesting."

Les drew two, equal, smaller circles under the first one.

"People who have split a home church in this way say that it feels like a divorce. Let's say Bob's home church is getting large enough to outgrow the living room, and some people are no longer participating as they did when it was smaller. Here's another option."

Les drew a small circle beside the original circle representing a home church, and an arrow going from the larger "church" to the smaller one.

"When a new person wants to join Bob's church, why not suggest that some people start a church at his house instead. That way, Bob's church has given birth to a daughter, rather than having a divorce. In fact, you don't have to wait until it's getting too big to birth a daughter church. If someone who seems like a 'person of peace' joins Bob's church, you could start one with him anyway."

"What is a person of peace? Jim asked.

"The concept comes from Luke 10, where Jesus sends out 70 of His disciples to the surrounding cities to prepare the way for Him to come. They are told to look for a person of peace. This person is open to hearing about the Lord. He has a circle of friends that he influences, and is willing to introduce you to them."

There was a pause in their conversation as the waitress served their food. The discussion continued as they ate.

"All over the world, God is using rapidly multiplying house churches to transform communities," explained Les. "The same could happen in this country, too! Simple churches are the obvious way to reach people who wouldn't darken the doors of a church building. But they will come into your home.

"I've brought a book for you that I have found very helpful. It's published by House2House and it's called Getting Started. It's a manual on how to start house churches. We've started more than a dozen churches by following the principles in it."

Les handed Bob a book with a cartoon on the front cover.

"Thanks, Les. I'll read it. It looks really interesting."

As their time together drew to a close, Les made a suggestion.

"Let's keep in regular touch on this. We could set up a monthly phone call so you can fill me in on how things are going. And if there's anything I can do to help, just let me know."

"I'd like that," said Jim. He thought for a moment.

"Does this mean that any churches I start have to be a part of your network?"

"No, not at all," replied Les. "I'm not trying to build up Harvest Home Church Network. This isn't about building my empire or organization or expanding my sphere of influence. You and I are friends! This thing isn't organization based, but relationship based. The apostle Paul was not an organizational figure in an early church hierarchy. Jesus is building His church. What's important is the Kingdom!

"Jim, I know this idea is contrary to all the church growth literature. This is your opportunity to expand the Kingdom and share Jesus. It's completely open and free. I believe the more I give it away, the more it will grow. You cannot out-give God!"

"Here, take my napkin teaching so you can refer to it."

Jim followed Les's advice. Three months after moving, he had started three churches!

"START TWELVE!"

Les was a pastor in a traditional church for 24 years. During that time, the church he pastored had home groups, cell groups, zone meetings, and topical meetings. He always recognized the importance of the intimacy and relationship that occurs in a smaller group setting. But these small meetings were always feeder groups into "real" church on Sunday morning.

He moved out of state to pastor a new church with cell meetings. But it wasn't fulfilling for people because of its inward-looking nature. The motivation for the cells was still to build a typical Sunday morning church service.

Les explains what happened next.

"Two to three years ago, I started meeting with other people in our area who are involved in house churches. I read *Houses that Change the World* by Wolfgang Simson and went to a house church conference, and my thinking began to change. The Lord spoke to me about the differences between a cell church and house churches.

"In a cell church, there is still very much an organizational hierarchy, and people follow the vision of the senior leadership. In a house or simple church, the leadership structure is flat or non-hierarchical, and it supports the vision God gives to the people in the churches.

"Things clicked!" says Les. "Then I came across a book called Simply Church and the Getting Started manual from House2House. The manual is helpful because it is practical. People can read it and say 'I can do that! I can't start a church if it requires $350,000, but I can do this. I can open up my home and meet with people.'"

A year ago, Les was planning three new churches. But one day, as he was praying, he sensed the Lord speaking to him.

"You are not to start three or four churches this year; that's your own thinking. You are going to start 12!"

Les has done that. Their network has actually started around 20 churches. A few of them have failed, but most are still going strong and people are becoming Christians. Some churches are local; some are out of state, like Jim's. They have started churches in a low-income housing project and in different neighborhoods. Twenty-five kids on the campus of the local university are on fire for the Lord. They are in the process of starting three more groups at the present time. One of the students recently married and transferred colleges, and is about to start something in their new home.

The leader of one of the churches in a subdivision feels strongly that he has been called to pastor the people who live in his neighborhood, whether they know the Lord or not. If they need help, he will seek to provide for them. For example, the church helped a single mother with three teenage kids to find furniture, and then gave them some money at Christmas time.

One of the churches met in a local restaurant for over a year until it outgrew the small room they rented. They sat around the table for a couple of hours and talked about the events of the past week and how they relate to prophecy. People come from a wide area to that meeting. They still have a good relationship with the owners of the restaurant and the waitresses, and often go there. Another Messianic group meets on a Friday night to celebrate the Jewish Sabbath.

Les quite frequently gives the Getting Started manual to people, and several churches have started that way. He finds it most effective to meet with a person to impart vision to them, and then gives them the manual to study. Regular follow up is important, too.

A number of these new churches are not connected to Les' network. Les helps people at any level, with no strings attached. He is intentionally holding back from organizing things because he wants Jesus to be the one building His church.

"We still have a Sunday morning congregational meeting, but its heart and purpose is not to get people to come to the Sunday meeting! We use it to train and disciple people to start churches. This is healthy! We're not about building a congregational meeting, but about expanding the Kingdom. If one day the government bans public meetings, then we can do without it. But for now, in our situation, we feel the Lord wants us to keep it.

"The majority of the people who are part of the house church don't necessarily come to the Sunday meeting. We see a phenomenon occurring in that many peoples' covenant relational connections are with the house church, not the Sunday congregational meeting. They might even go to a different church on a Sunday. One family goes to a traditional church on Sunday so their kids can go to Sunday School, but the house church is their real church—and they know it!"

Les's network of simple churches is called Harvest Home Church Network. But Harvest is part of a regional network of networks. Four different networks make up Sojourners, which includes 30 to 40 simple churches. The leaders get together regularly, and they all have the same heart to see their area transformed.

Les has a pastor's heart. He loves to train leaders to pastor their groups effectively. He tells them, "Just keep in touch with people in a simple way. Find out how they are doing. Know what's going on in their lives because of relationship, not because you are sitting in an office, going down a list and mechanically calling people.

"I can't say I'm not tempted, but I know that I'm not called to be a famous international speaker. I serve in the corner of the vineyard where God has placed me and I do what He's asking me to do. I don't see it as a springboard to fame and fortune."

Perhaps because he is so secure in where God has him, Les likes to zero in on a person's security—that they know their calling and gifting from God.

"When I see someone interested in starting a church in their home, I look to see how secure they are in themselves and in their walk with God. If they are not secure as a person, they're not as likely to be fruitful. But if they are secure and just want to share the Lord with other people, they are likely to be very fruitful. One brother shared his concern that if we send a new believer into the domain of darkness to interface with the world, they won't present a good example of Jesus. But I find that if they are secure in the Lord, (and this might happen in a few days—they don't have to be a Christian for 20 years or go to seminary), they can share their faith and start a church."

Les would like to see fruitful church workers released from their secular jobs to work full time in the Kingdom.

"The Lord still intends to fulfill the priesthood of all believers as Martin Luther saw it. If 100 new leaders were released to work full time, the Kingdom would expand more quickly. Satan is after the "layhood of all believers," that none should be released full time. In recognizing how wasteful it is to spend so much money on buildings and clergy who view salaries as an entitlement, we have gone too far the other way. I'm not saying that all believers will end up in full-time ministry. But there's room for 100 times more Ephesians 4 people operating trans-locally to work full time in the Kingdom."

KEY THOUGHTS: NO EMPIRE BUILDING, NO CONTROL AND NO GLORY

Les loves to give away what he is learning. He is not trying to expand his circle of influence or build his own little kingdom. God's Kingdom is far more important to him.

A few years ago, the Lord gave us a "triple slogan" which we long to characterize this movement of simple, organic churches.

"No empire building,
No control,
No glory!"

At House2House magazine, we quite frequently get calls from people asking us if they can join House2House.

"I'm sorry, but there's nothing to join," we say. "We'll do everything we can to help you, but there's no House2House network of churches."

Too often, people measure success in God's Kingdom by the world's standards. They are interested in numbers, in (church) political power and in influence.

It would be so easy for us here at House2House to build our own empire, but we are determined we will not do that. For fear of being tempted to somehow claim credit for them, we don't even want to keep track of the number of churches across the country that start as a result of the magazine or other writing and conferences,. We don't trust ourselves with that kind of information. Our desire is to build Jesus' Kingdom. (The Lord is leading some others to keep closer track of their national networks. After all, someone on the Day of Pentecost had the forethought to count how many people were baptized. That is great; we are only saying He is not leading us that way.)

Control is of similar concern. Too many of our legacy churches are dominated by power struggles and control issues. "The people in the pew cannot be trusted to hear God for themselves." "The only vision that counts is that of the senior pastor or the leadership team." Whose church is this? It belongs to Jesus! He is the one building His church. He can be trusted to lead His people. And we can expect His people to hear Him.

In these simpler expressions of church, we long for Jesus to be the one in control. If someone hears the Holy Spirit speaking to them and telling them a course of action, our response should be, "What can we do to support you? Do you need any resources? How can we help?"

The apostle Paul quite frequently left a church (because he was thrown out of town) after just a few days or weeks (e.g. Philippi, Thessalonica or Berea). From that point on, he visited infrequently and communicated with them by letter. He was content to leave the church under the control of the Holy Spirit. Let's trust the Holy Spirit.

No glory! How often have the lives of charismatic leaders within God's Kingdom been shipwrecked because they have taken God's glory for themselves? They are willing to let the fame and honor rub off on them. They delight in being praised, and eagerly accept the applause and accolades of others.

But can any of us say fame wouldn't affect us the same way? Only the Lord can keep our attitudes right; we cannot do it ourselves. Lord, don't let us touch Your glory!

The history of various moves of God reveals that it isn't long before people start to take over—creating programs and plans that put God in a box and replacing the Holy Spirit with their own strategies and good ideas. Will this one be any different? Will we, as a movement, be able to resist the temptation to act as God?

"God, have mercy on us!"

TONY & FELICITY'S STORY

(Part 2)

The bigger picture

HOUSE2HOUSE

In late 2000, two leaders from other networks of simple churches in central Texas approached us. Jim and David are good friends we have been working with for several years.

"We have a vision for a magazine for the house-church movement," Jim shared with us. "Would you be willing to join us?"

We saw the value of a magazine back in the British house-church movement. Further research showed us that many of the major moves of God over countless decades were somehow "represented" by a magazine. The magazine often acted as a catalyst to further the work of God.

We not only joined with Jim and David in their vision, we soon found ourselves carrying primary responsibility for the day-to-day running of the magazine called *House2House*. Much to our delight and amazement, the magazine has captured people's imaginations, and now is sent all over the world. It is an incredible (and humbling) privilege for us, because it means that people contact us to let us know what God is doing in their area. We receive emails or phone calls from people on a daily basis, and the most frequent comment we get is this:

"God led us to have church in our home, but we thought we were the only ones doing church that way. Then we came across the magazine, and we discovered that God is doing this all over the country and across the world. We are part of a move of God's Spirit. We're not alone any longer!"

Some of our thinking about simple churches over the years has been influenced by a book manuscript that initially could only be

245

downloaded from the Internet. Called *Houses that Change the World*, it is written by a German researcher, Wolfgang Simson. During our first visit to India, we had the opportunity to meet Wolfgang. We spent an afternoon with him and were impressed by the extent and clarity of his thinking about the nature of the church. (And we thought we were radical!)

"Wolfgang, would you be willing to come to the States and speak to us and some of our friends?" we asked him.

Wolfgang accepted our invitation, and the date was set for March 2001.

We sent out a few emails and invited people to a Saturday conference in our home. It wasn't long before we wondered if we had bitten off more than we could chew. We got the definite impression that more people were coming than we had anticipated.

"Should we move the conference to a church building?" we wondered. We eventually decided to leave it in our home (after all, this was a conference on home church), and we begged and borrowed extra chairs everywhere we could think of.

In the end, over 160 came! (Luckily our home has an open floor plan, and we actually managed to seat everyone. Our septic system did not cope quite as well, but that is another story!) Wolfgang shared with authority and many were challenged. But the friendships with others of like mind across the country—many of which have been strategic—were perhaps the most important thing to come out of the day.

It shouldn't have surprised us, but Satan did not appreciate what was going on. The very month we committed to the magazine, the only major client in our business took work in-house that we were doing for them. By this time, we were running a business in the area of medical cost containment. We were forced to let go some of our staff, a very painful procedure since they were our close friends. It took us a few months to realize what was going on.

"This is spiritual warfare," we decided. "How could we not have seen it before?"

As soon as we grasped the situation, we determined to pray it through. The weekend that we finally understood what was happening, we took every opportunity we could to head to the office to pray.

Anyone who saw us there would have thought we were crazy! We did everything we knew in the area of spiritual warfare. We sang, we marched and shouted, we declared victory, we fought against demonic hordes, we claimed God's promises of provision and we quoted Scripture. On the following Monday morning, we had a breakthrough. A potential client was interested in us.

It took months before we were solvent again, and years before the business was profitable. But in these last few years, we have learned how to wage spiritual warfare on a daily basis. It's far more than coincidence that whenever we take the time to fight spiritually, we see our business advance. But if we let the prayer slide, nothing happens. In God's economy, losing a major client was one of the best things that could have happened to us because of the lessons we learned. For some years, we asked the Lord to help us be strategic within the Kingdom; obviously the most strategic thing we can do is pray. Now we are trying to apply the principles we have learned on spiritual warfare to what is happening across the nation.

For several years, the network of churches we started has taken the opportunity provided by the long Labor Day weekend to go on a retreat together. We initially used an old ranch house in the middle of nowhere. We enjoyed the beautiful countryside, and someone came to share from the Lord with us. As numbers increased, we graduated to a hotel in a nearby city. When we opened the conference up to readers of the magazine, it grew considerably. People from all over the country now attend the National House Church Conference and speakers share what God is saying to the movement as a whole.

LUKE 10

We have also started a course on how to begin churches with those who are not yet Christians. Called "Luke 10," the concept originally was Wolfgang's brainchild.

We conducted the first Luke 10 course in our home three years ago over a series of six weekends with people from our surrounding area. The course is designed to help people who want to start simple or house churches, and we look at many of the principles involved.

Since then, we have run several in our home over six days with people from around the country. The events have been characterized by an amazing sense of the Lord's presence, and a freedom for the Holy Spirit to move. And churches have started as a result.

The obvious limitation of running things in our home is that not many people can take off work for six days. The Lord then gave us the idea of adapting to Luke 10 Online, which allows more people to participate and is reproducible. At the beginning of every Luke 10 course in our home, we told the Lord that unless He shows up, this course is a waste of time. And He never disappointed us! As we started offering the courses online, we were concerned we wouldn't experience that same sense of the Holy Spirit doing whatever He wanted. However, our experience online so far has been that the Holy Spirit shows up in power!

The Luke 10 course is based on the *Getting Started* manual, with an emphasis on practical experience in the principles being taught. We have condensed it somewhat for Luke 10 Online, to hone in on those aspects of the course that are relevant to starting churches, especially with unbelievers. In Luke 10 Online, a coach works via conference call with a group of facilitators from around the country, each of whom has a local group. Teaching is done primarily through various practical activities, but also by CD or MP3 and email. Homework reinforces the lessons learned. In fact, since people taking the online course practice a concept during the week, they are starting even more churches than those who went through it in our home.

We are making the materials available for smaller groups to use on their own as a *Getting Started* course.

It also has been a great privilege working with a team of like-minded visionaries from across the country. We stay accountable to one another. We have been looking at what to do if and when the concept of house or simple, organic churches reaches a tipping point in this country. (The tipping point occurs when an idea becomes acceptable across a wide spectrum of society.) I remember sitting in a meeting when a dozen or so of us came together to wait on the Lord for two days.

"How will we avoid the 'superstar mentality'?" someone asked. "When simple churches gain acceptance, people are bound to want to put a charismatic personality on a pedestal, and that's the last thing we want. Is there a way to prevent it?"

"It's not that the movement won't have leadership," added another. "But leadership has to be non-hierarchical—a humble servant seeking the good of others, not seeking the limelight."

"Maybe we should make sure that any media attention is shared between all of us," suggested one. "If, for example, someone is featured in a magazine article, and that leads to increased publicity, the next time they get asked, they should say, 'Oh I'm not the person you want to speak to! You should talk to so and so!'"

Since that discussion, this actually has happened!

We have also been thinking through how to prevent simple churches from becoming just another church growth program as the concept gains acceptance. Although it might have an initial measure of success, if something is done as a method rather than from the Holy Spirit, it will not produce the move of the Holy Spirit we all long for. Prayer is probably the only recourse we have on that one!

It is becoming obvious that God is moving in this nation and across the Western world. We may not have the numbers yet, but we no longer have to go to Asia or Africa to see His hand at work. All over the country, God is leading His people to meet simply, in their homes or their places of work. The movement is very outward-focused with an emphasis on reaching unbelievers. It is also gaining the attention of church and denominational leaders, many who are in contact with us or others we work with and are wondering how they can get involved.

The magazine gives us a front seat in the arena of what God is doing with simple, organic churches across the Western world. The stories of what is happening are incredible! God is on the move!

KEY THOUGHTS: THE BIGGER PICTURE

For various reasons, church as we have always known it is becoming increasingly irrelevant in today's fast-paced society. Each week, thousands are leaving our legacy churches, never to return.

In his thought- provoking book *The Present Future*, Reggie McNeal reveals that we are seeing a new phenomenon in the United States today. For the first time in history, people are leaving the traditional church in order to preserve their faith. In fact, the fastest growing segment of the church today is that of Christians outside the church. The majority of them are mature, seasoned Christians. Many of them are no longer isolated and insulated from the rest of the world. They are an army, trained and available. What will happen when they catch a vision of multiplying simple churches?

Those in leadership across the denominations are becoming increasingly aware that the church in this country is in a state of serious decline. Unless something changes, we are only one generation away from being a post-Christian society such as Europe, where Christianity has long since ceased being significant. These leaders can see that the vast majority of churches are not growing, and that we are not even managing to keep up with the rate of population growth. As they seek the Lord's face for answers, many of these leaders are coming to the conclusion that the answer lies in simpler forms of church—just as in the rest of the world. These churches are led by ordinary people rather than professionals, with an emphasis on reaching out to the world. Could they train and release their people to go out into their spheres of influence, make disciples and start churches as part of their church's outreach efforts?

When the Bible was put into the hands of ordinary people back in the 1500s, the result was the Reformation. This did more than merely change the church; it transformed nations. In the same way the man in the pew gained hold of the Bible "back then," what could happen if the church was released into the hands of ordinary people today? Another Reformation could be on the way.

There is an increasing hunger in this nation for an authentic spirituality. The signs are everywhere. Look in any bookstore or at a movie or TV guide. The fields are ripe and ready to harvest. The majority of workers for the harvest may come from that harvest. As people within this new movement of God become disciples, a part of their DNA will be to multiply.

This nation will be transformed only as an army of ordinary people are willing to get out of their comfortable pews or arm-chairs to tell the world the good news: Jesus still heals the sick and sets the captives free. When ordinary Christians say "Yes" to God and move out into their neighborhoods or their work-place to make disciples and start simple churches among those who are not yet Christians, we will see a spectacular advance in the Kingdom.

This army of ordinary believers is already mobilizing. The Western world is about to see what happens when the ordinary believer goes into action for the Kingdom.

You, too, could have a story like the ones in this book.

Are you ready to enlist?

Do you have a story?

*We'd like to offer you an invitation
to share it with us at:*

www. AnArmyofOrdinaryPeople.com.

APPENDIX

PARADIGM SHIFTS–CHANGES IN OUR THINKING

Over the past decade, as Tony and I have traveled along this path of simple, organic or house church, certain concepts have totally altered the way we live or think about and practice church—once we have truly grasped them.

Here are the main ones:

1. Church genuinely is "where two or three are gathered together in His name." This understanding of church turned our lives upside down. When we realized that church was neither buildings nor meetings, but relationship with Jesus and with His people, it meant that church occurred when we came together with others on a daily basis. We are church when we are together in His name. We are not church just because we are in a special building at a special time with special people leading us. Not only that, anyone can start a church if it is just a few friends coming together!

2. Jesus is to be the head of His church. This is not mere theory, but must be lived out in practice in our everyday lives together.

3. Simple is reproducible, complex is not. Most churches are all about raising the bar, creating a higher standard, whether that is in leadership, teaching or worship. Simple church is about lowering the bar, making it possible for everyone to get involved.

4. Churches are meant to multiply. Every living thing God has created reproduces after its kind. God hates barrenness. Churches are not meant to be sterile. There are more than 50 commands in the New Testament that include the words "one another." These commands can only be obeyed within a small-group context. We need to multiply the small, not look to grow ever larger. If we are getting to a size where these commands cannot be obeyed, it's time to multiply!

5. The resources are in the harvest. The "person of peace" principle means that workers for a particular segment of society are to be found within that people group or subculture. It means that if a person becomes a Christian, we do not automatically invite them to our church. We prefer to start a church in their house with the people in their sphere of influence.

   If the resources are in the harvest, it means that our next generation of leaders may not even be Christians yet. We love watching a person become a Christian, introduce their friends to Jesus, and end up leading a church under the mentorship of a more mature believer.

6. Non-religious Christianity. Christianity is not meant to be a rule book, a series of laws for which we are punished if we break them. When we become Christians, God gives us new hearts of flesh with His laws written on them. If we live from our hearts, spontaneously, we will find ourselves living a life that is pleasing to Him. We no longer have to color inside the lines. God is not sitting up in heaven with a big stick waiting to catch us in some sin. A life lived from the heart is very attractive to unbelievers

7. The priesthood of all believers. We are a Kingdom of priests. (I Peter 2:9) All the members of the body of Christ are important. Each of us can have direct connection to our Head, Jesus. We no longer need an intermediary to go to the throne room for us. It's time for the clergy/laity distinction

to end.

This is not a mere theological truth. It needs to become a practical reality in our lives together. When we get together, each of us is meant to take part. Each one of us has a contribution to make to our shared lives. (I Corinthians 14:26)

8. Leadership is servanthood. Jesus meant it when He said leadership within His Kingdom is not like leadership in the world. He gave us a practical example of how it should look when He washed His disciples' feet. Jesus literally laid down His life for others. Our lives need to reflect His attitude of servanthood.

WHERE DO YOU GO FROM HERE?

If the concepts presented through these stories grabbed your attention, and if you are sensing the Lord may want you to take these ideas further, here are some suggestions for you as you seek the Lord:

Books to read:

Houses that Change the World	Wolfgang Simson
Simply Church	Tony and Felicity Dale
Getting Started	Felicity Dale
The Global House Church Movement	Rad Zdero
Church Planting Movements	David Garrison
Saturation Church Planting	Robert Fitts
Organic Church	Neil Cole
Megashift	James Rutz

Websites:

House2House magazine	www.house2house.net
Dawn Ministries (North America)	www.dawnministries.org

Videos:

Church Planting Movements: available from the International Mission Board of the Southern Baptist Convention at www.imb.org. Watch Out - A Tidal Wave Is Coming: available from www.house2house.net.

Further training:

Luke 10 Online or Getting Started courses	www.house2house.net
Greenhouse	www.cmaresources.org

If you have found this book helpful,
the following resources by
Tony and Felicity Dale
(available from www.house2house.net)
may interest you:

Simply Church:
In this book, Tony and Felicity explore some dynamic trends in society and church that are pushing believers into simpler ways of doing church. It gets back to basics by bringing it all back to the Lord. It's Simply Church.

Getting Started:
We all recognize it would be ludicrous to think that nailing a steeple to the roof of a house would make it a house church. However, many of us take what we've seen happen in church buildings our whole lives, duplicate it in our living room and call it a church. Simple church is not about a change of location; it's about a change in the way we do church. This practical manual will help you change the way you view church and church planting.

The Getting Started Course:
This six-week course helps people experience the Getting Started manual in a practical, small group setting. Learning from DVDs, CDs and through various practical activities, the course is ideal for groups of 4 to 12 people working together to learn the basics of church planting. The focus is on starting new communities of faith among those who don't know the Lord personally.

The Luke 10 Training Course:
Tony and Felicity have a burden to help provide practical training for those who have a heart to reach non-Christians. One of the most effective ways of doing this is establishing simple/organic churches with groups of people who do not yet know Christ. In Luke 10 Online, a coach works via conference call with a group of facilitators from around the country. Teaching is done primarily using practical activities, but also by CD or MP3 and email.

We also encourage you to sign up for the free e-letter and *House2House* Magazine so you can keep up with the rapid growth of simple churches nationwide.
Go to **www.house2house.net** to get more information, sign up for the e-letter and magazine and to purchase the resources described above.

AUTHOR BIOGRAPHY

Tony and Felicity Dale certainly aren't rookies when it comes to being in the thick of church-planting movements. While receiving their medical training at Barts Hospital in London in the mid-70s, the Dales were active in the British House Church movement, pioneering a church in their medical college and later in the East End of London.

In 1987, the Dales moved to the United States, where they developed businesses to support themselves and again jumped heart-first into church planting. Out of these church-starting pursuits, the vision and relationships developed that led to the formation of House2House magazine. They also have authored several books, including: Renewing the Mind, Simply Church and the Getting Started Manual on planting house churches.

Printed in the United States
54145LVS00007B/124-144